The Newcomer Student

The Newcomer Student

An Educator's Guide to Aid Transitions

Louise H. Kreuzer

ROWMAN & LITTLEFIELD
Lanham • Boulder • New York • London

Published by Rowman & Littlefield
A wholly owned subsidiary of The Rowman & Littlefield Publishing Group, Inc.
4501 Forbes Boulevard, Suite 200, Lanham, Maryland 20706
www.rowman.com

Unit A, Whitacre Mews, 26-34 Stannary Street, London SE11 4AB

British Library Cataloguing in Publication Information Available

Library of Congress Cataloging-in-Publication Data

Names: Kreuzer, Louise H., author.
Title: The newcomer student: an educator's guide to aid transitions / Louise H. Kreuzer.
Description: Lanham, Maryland: Rowman & Littlefield, 2016. | Includes bibliographical
  references and index.
Identifiers: LCCN 2015046208 (print) | LCCN 2016006431 (ebook) |
  ISBN 9781475825589 (cloth : alk. paper) | ISBN 9781475825596 (pbk. : alk. paper) |
  ISBN 9781475825602 (Electronic)
Subjects: LCSH: Refugees—Education—United States. | Immigrants—Education—
  United States.
Classification: LCC LC3731 .K74 2016 (print) | LCC LC3731 (ebook) |
  DDC 371.826/914—dc23
LC record available at http://lccn.loc.gov/2015046208

Printed in the United States of America

To Daddy, for always believing I could reach the moon.
To Cathryne Louise Acree, for being my lighthouse and my
safe place in the world. You are my inspiration for all things
good and strong. You are loved beyond measure.

Contents

Acknowledgments

No part of this endeavor would have been possible without the combined support and council of key influential figures. These individuals have profoundly impacted my personal and professional growth in overwhelmingly positive ways. I am deeply grateful for their selfless efforts and guidance, which ultimately led to the culmination of this text.

To begin, I would like to thank my immediate family. Betsy, Mark, Bud, David, Teresa, Melissa, Davis, and Tobey—you have been sources of unending support and guidance. Danielle, my dear sister, you are, as always, my port in the storm, my lever of truth, and my inspiration for all things beautiful.

Professionally, I am indebted foremost to my mentor Dr. Margaret Rohan, who happens to be a veritable expert in the arena of Newcomer education. Despite her long list of credentials, she calls herself a peer in our shared workplace. Without her knowledge and aid, this text would be without meat or marrow. More than this, Margaret is the most rare brand of friend, unwavering in her devotion and generosity. Thank you for being a lighthouse, in more ways than you can imagine.

Also, the following credits are due: Brenda Kazin, Ken Hansen and the Place Bridge Academy team, for allowing me the opportunity to practice my craft in such a remarkably diverse and fulfilling setting; Dr. Fredoline Anunobi for guiding the Fulbright-Hayes to Tanzania endeavor, an experience that would prove life-affecting in every regard; and the Rodel Award team, for believing in my worth and matching me with my first professional mentor, the remarkable Kathy Puryear.

Additional thanks to Richard and Susan Kreuzer for being the kindest of souls and the most professional of proofreaders; to Daniel Tijerina for providing design council and creative advice; and to Zahi Yaafouri for his ongoing encouragement.

Writing of this text occurred predominately in two locations, both of which permanently transformed my personal and professional self. For my time at Black Mountain Ranch, I am obliged to the May family. For my extended time in Tanzania, I am grateful to many, including the Dzombe and Sudi families and the U.S. Embassy.

Finally, to Hani Yaafouri, my best friend and dedicated partner, I am infinitely blessed for your presence and calm measure. I deeply appreciate your acting as a true champion for my ambitions, even as they comprise our immediate ease. You are a teacher of balance and unflinching morality, and I am a better person for knowing you. Thank you for opening the doors to your culture and inviting me in. We are rich for knowing that wherever we are together, we are home.

The teaching craft is reliant upon the "it-takes-a-village" mentality. The Newcomer teaching sector requires this type of cohesiveness on a grand and exaggerated scale. Similarly, the processes of day-to-day life (and writing, I have learned) also require combined cooperation. None of us is an island. We are all in this together, as teachers, as Americans, as global citizens.

This text is the culmination of life experiences, relentless determination, and the efforts of all those around me. I consider myself exponentially blessed to be surrounded with such extraordinary mentors, guides, leaders, fellow teachers, friends, and loved ones. Truly and with all of my heart, I applaud you.

Foreword

It was June, 2012. There we were, my daughter Kate and I, totally awed by a welcoming procession of young learners at the "Never Give Up" Education Center in Morogoro, Tanzania. It was a profound moment we hold in our minds that keeps us inspired every day of our lives. We were mere ambassadors for Louise Kreuzer, who had received a Fulbright Scholarship to study in Tanzania two years prior. Kreuzer founded this school and developed an organization, P.E.A.C.E. Project Africa, a non-profit organization providing free and rigorous education to students in a sustainable, eco-responsible learning environment. Since then, she has been awarded the honor of Denver's "Teacher of the Year" in 2012, and continues to do extensive research . . . *The Newcomer Student: An Educator's Guide to Aid Transitions* being the result.

The power of this book, and the reason you want to read it, is how Kreuzer innovates new educational approaches based on genuine experience, as she embodies current theoretical practice. With a foundation of strong research, this reference guide comprises the missing piece in ELL educational material, that being the cultural history, the long, complex, immigrant journey and its insurmountable odds. Detailed also are the legal hurdles encountered, and emotional background each Newcomer brings to the Twenty-First Century classroom. After reading the domains of culture shock and the expectations of Newcomer behavior, educators will put this book down better prepared to be not just effective, but also compassionate. With the caring and sensitivity of an artist, Kreuzer integrates intellectual rigor with practical application of activities.

This guide is the launching point that invites every educator to link the West with the East . . . and the rest of the world, on the ultimate meeting ground–schools. The importance of parent involvement being a big invest-ment, recognizing the shared, fundamental values, with great payoffs, and ways to achieve that through a variety of parent meeting venues, are included. Of particular interest are the Cultural Nuances, such as 'saving face,' eye con-tact, touching the head, facial expressions and hand gestures, every teacher will appreciate knowing. There are international calendars of important dates, international tongue twisters, and fascinating global proverbs.

The Newcomer Learner would be incomplete if it did not describe theories regarding second language acquisition and how they have emerged, which it does thoroughly. In addition, there is an inclusion of the WIDA Can Do Descriptors, which are so vitally important in assessing the students, who have rich learning experiences . . . just in different languages! Enhancing this read are relevant quotes, flowcharts, graphic organizers and student samples. There are detailed descriptions of many specific, practical, step-by-step activ-ities in physical expression, musical extensions and what sheltered instruction looks like. There are instructional methods in academic vocabulary strategies, co-operative structures, the usefulness of visual cues and textile manipula-tion. Storytelling is highlighted because it fosters oral and written expression, and develops writing skills. The retelling of personal experiences creates a fertile ground for self-discovery, social understanding and makes sense of poignant life events. Literacy is imbedded into cross-curriculum activities, with suggested lists of age-level multicultural books by world region.

All making you the expert . . . Kreuzer's definitive intention.

In reading *The Newcomer Learner*, you will realize that finding balance in supporting host language growth and heritage language preservation is crucial in authentic learning. Coming from an asset based, rather than deficit, point of view, this book includes a discussion of assets such as commu-nication, creativity, flexibility, critical thinking, self-initiative, leadership, accountability and productivity, technology and social fluidity.

The reader cannot dismiss how Newcomer education provides opportuni-ties for personal and professional transformation and consequently, change. Kreuzer takes the idea of "making a difference" to new heights. Above all, her writing style is inspirational, compelling and visionary. She forces us to hold our students at the heart of our craft. She has provided the ultimate exemplar of a thoroughly efficient instructional and thoughtful program manual for teaching the Newcomer learner, with verve.

Recommended reading for pre-service teachers in undergraduate and graduate teacher training programs, *The Newcomer Learner* contains lan-guage and indispensible information for all who work with these amazing students . . . whether you are a neophyte or veteran educator, ECE instructor or school superintendent, community project liaison or post-settlement service provider. The powerful and dynamic contents of this book and its author will lead any humanitarian or educational program, into the Twenty-First Century classroom, where whole worlds collaborate.

Margaret A. Rohan

Unit I

EMBRACING THE
NEWCOMER LEARNER

Chapter 1

Acknowledging the Refugee Experience

الاعتراف تجربة اللاجئين- Arabic

ANY CLASSROOM, AN ELLIS ISLAND

At any given moment in the twenty-first century, more than ten million refugees are documented worldwide; and nearly half are children.[1] Over 41 million immigrants lived in the United States in 2013.[2] The specific needs of individual persons and families are vast and varied, as they transition to life in a new country. A successful relationship between a host nation and an asylum seeker is largely contingent upon the quantity and quality available of accessible aid services. This includes us, the educators, who will welcome and guide Newcomer learners in the host environment.

En route to a place on our classroom rosters, the resettled refugee or immigrant child will have coursed through an intricate system of relocation mechanisms and endured innumerable transformations. Refugee and immigrant families often endure multiple relocations, endless interviews, and a myriad of mental and physical assessments on the path to resettlement. They might have also experienced unimaginable distress: loss, sacrifice, hunger, human atrocity, and an exceptional scarcity of basic needs.

Resettlement histories are the ballads of a conflicted mankind, and testimonies of human migration are rarely short and sweet. Rather, they are elaborate, winding, uncomfortable testaments to the greatness of character and spirit. A very small percentage of those roads lead directly into our classrooms.

These "Newcomer" learners, as they are resettled into westernized regions, require a tailored brand of education. *In most academic settings, the term*

3

"Newcomer" applies to any learner whose presence in the host country amounts to one year or less; and who is, or will be, receiving educational services in a language other than their native tongue. The Newcomer framework for learning is grounded in the same high-expectation principles that apply to typical mainstream education. In addition to the academic component, it must also provide for explicit and exceptional interventions across a spectrum of need levels, including cultural, emotional, psychological, and biological prerequisites to host environment learning.

The Newcomer framework calls for certain key requirements. First, it is focused on accelerated host language acquisition, which is achieved through the implementation of language development scaffolds and sheltered instruction techniques. Next, it relies upon whole staff participation and necessitates teachers' conscientious evaluation of biased thinking and behavior patterns, such that the school organism is equipped to establish and maintain a healthy school wide climate. When this is achieved, heritage language and culture are valued; critical relationships between students, parents, and educators are nourished; and learners are empowered in their growth endeavors.

The core of Newcomer learning is, of course, stoutly scholastic. Learning, in its various forms, calls for a multitude of needs: exposure, trial, error, re-application and practice, practice, practice. For a Newcomer student, learning is an extended process that comes with what can be best described as an extended-extended process . . . and that's what's required just to get by.

In terms of immediate urgency, physical and emotional stability must be established as essential prerequisites for learning and pro-social successes. Next, language acquisition and development are the primary focus. The language piece alone is an impressive undertaking, typically requiring between three to seven years of dedicated practice to establish fluency.[3]

Beyond these initial layers of Newcomer learning awaits a new series of hurdles that are largely related to social efficacy. Expected sociocultural fluency incorporates a thorough grasp of normative behaviors pertaining to food, customs, holidays, hygienic protocol, dress, interactive conduct, and measures of discipline in the new setting. It also encompasses other real life skills in the host setting, such as bill paying, transportation, translation, home affairs, and childcare. Finally, we have the *drama* element—peer interaction, friendship, playground crushes, bullying, social media, and family-child relationships.

And, after all this, homework?!

WHO IS A REFUGEE?

Newcomers are often defined by a long and complicated series of statistics: data scores, influx patterns, poverty analyses, and of course, school performance grades. Certain figures are certainly useful and valid. But they lead us away from the relatable, tangible person. The relatable, tangible *student*; the learner we show up for. This leads us to the *who*.

In elementary talk, *human seeking refuge* is the main idea of the refugee story. Refugees are individuals with palpable faces and names who are colored by real life stories, experiences, families, and successes. Refugees and immigrants, akin to our host-nation selves, are people—parents, children, adventurers, workers, dreamers, teachers, students, feelers, believers, doers, and learners.

Again, like us, refugee individuals and families carry with them other things: tribulations, stressors, and personal legacies. Some family fabrics are cohesive; others show wear. Some individuals appear well adjusted and decodable, while others are stalemated in secrets, burdens, and internalized fears.

These pieces, combined, highlight one simple, beautiful, extraordinary truth. We are all *human*. Each of us is susceptible, and yet, each of us is a channel for resiliency. We are all magnificent and full of promise, just as we are tarnished and unsteady. Each of us owns an access point to greatness. More than this, we all possess the inherent ability to help and guide one another through processes of personal and contextual transformation.

Let's think this through. Are we, as westernized Americans in our own subjective neighborhoods, so exempt from characteristics of trial, loss, joy, confusion, relocation, or overcoming? Of course not! Sure, some of our stories register relatively low on the scale of global severity. Nevertheless, our personal tribulations and successes are meaningful to us, within the context and perimeters of life as we are familiar with it. No story is insignificant.

Greatness belongs to each of us.

WHO IS ELIGIBLE FOR REFUGEE STATUS?

Any person who is forced to flee their native country out of legitimate fear for personal safety and well-being may register as a refugee.[4,5] There are more than 1 million registered refugees in the world at any given time. Thousands more exist unregistered.[6] The United Nations High Commissioner for Refugees (UNHCR) qualifies a refugee individual as one whom "owing to a well-founded fear of being persecuted for reasons of race, religion, nationality, membership of a particular social group or political opinion, is outside the country of his nationality, and is unable to, or owing to such fear, is unwilling to avail himself of the protection of that country."[7]

Receiving nations have strict protocols for qualifying refugees for resettlement. To begin with, refugee-status accessibility must be limited, so as not to overwhelm a nation's resource capacities. In the United States, the Presidential Determination declares a target threshold for asylum seekers each year. In a second annual objective, the U.S. president, in conjunction with Congress, assigns a set of "preferential" origination locales, or global regions for heightened U.S. attention.[8] Beyond these foundational stipulations, additional checkpoints are in place. In the United States, for example, refugee-status applicants must satisfy specific criteria. A potentially qualifying applicant, according to the International Rescue Committee, will:

- [Adhere to] the definition of a "refugee" as determined by U.S. government officials.
- Be among those refugees determined by the president to be of special humanitarian concern to the United States.
- Be otherwise admissible under U.S. law.
- Not be firmly resettled in any foreign country.

The organization also notes that, "although a refugee may meet the above criteria, the existence of the U.S. Refugee Admissions Program does not create any entitlement for that person to be admitted to the U.S."[9,10] In short, there are no guarantees. Opportunities for refugee relocation to third-party host zones are scant; resettlement to "first nation" host territories, exceptional.

As professional educators, we like to remind our students of their uniqueness. "You're one in a million," we recite. Perhaps, with regard to our Newcomer students, we simply couldn't speak a more prominent truth. Really. . . one in a million.

LIFE IN A REFUGEE HAVEN

It is the human saga: in times of turmoil, we flee areas of risk in search of safety and comfort. We have entered a new era of problem solving in this regard. For the first time in history, persecuted persons may be eligible for relocation aid, via sources that may be entirely unrelated by culture, language, or proximity.[11]

Today, networks of government and nongovernmental institutions are prepared to assume the task of ensuring human safety. These organizations assist in temporarily or permanently relocating displaced individuals and entire families to refugee camps within allocated "safe" zones. In this new world, the displaced person is redefined. He or she is a sanctioned refugee.

It is difficult to capture the essence and extent of what a refugee camp actually is. Refugee settlements are not typically self-supporting, and rely extensively on external aid for nearly all matters of finance, food, health, and viability. They are notoriously unglamorous, routinely undersupplied, and statistically dangerous. The UN High Commission for Refugees offers that, "Refugee camp is a term used to describe human settlements which vary greatly in size and character. In general, refugee camps are enclosed areas, restricted to refugees and those assisting them, where protection and assistance is provided until it is safe for the refugees to return to their home or to be resettled elsewhere."[12]

POINT A TO Z: MAPPING TRANSITION

Refugee relocation requires multiparty participation. In the United States, there are several baseline entities responsible for the selection and details of resettlement. They include: the U.S. Resettlement Program (USRP); international U.S. Embassies; the Department of State's Bureau for Population, Refugees and Migration (PRM); and the office of United States Citizenship and Immigration Services (USCIS).

The path to resettlement is an extensive and complicated one. First, candidates for refugee status must be referred by the UNHCR or the U.S. Embassy in the designated area. Generally, whole families are referred at once. Incredibly, only 1 percent of the world's refugee population will be referred for U.S. Refugee Status.[13]

The PRM manages refugee influx into the United States at the most fundamental level. It is responsible for managing the U.S. Refugee Admissions Program, and works directly with foreign U.S. embassies to accomplish its aims. At the heart of the PRM's widespread duties, its central focus is to coordinate and facilitate appropriate global rearrangement according to critical mass human needs at a precise given moment.

In many cases, this will involve sanctuary-seeking relocation efforts. Additionally, the State Department defines application criteria for refugees. The agency is also responsible for establishing our nation's target hosting capacity for a given fiscal duration, and determines the countries that will receive preferential refugee intake for a given year.[14]

The next entity linked to immigrant and refugee resettlement in America is the United States Citizenship and Immigration Services (USCIS) unit. Ultimately, USCIS is the terminus for all foreigner stay in the United States. The USCIS oversees the most detailed processes of refugee and immigrant resettlement. These include interviews, fingerprinting, background checks, biometrics, sponsorship, and all processing for all supporting documentation. USCIS is also the issuing agency for VISA, Green Card, and U.S. citizenship status. Each of these accomplishments can require months or years to realize.[15]

In addition to its home-based duties, the USCIS maintains a unique set of foreign duties. Specifically, agents from this organization routinely travel to various international regions, with the purpose of screening, interviewing, and preparing candidates for asylum. The offices of USCIS operate in tandem with a multitude of governmental and nongovernmental agencies to negotiate safe havens for individuals and families in need.

Only if the individual or family qualifies for refugee status under U.S. law, a USCIS agent will travel to the country of asylum to interview the intended persons. USCIS agents routinely visit distressed nations in an effort to determine refugee eligibility for refugee-status transfer to the United States. Immigration officers are dispatched to priority regions as determined by the U.S. central government. Inside the target zones, USCIS representatives must ascertain the degree to which an individual or family qualifies for refugee stay, as dictated by Federal law. Such determinations are achieved by a variety of means, including personal interviews, health screenings, and records verification.

Most transfer-eligible refugees are referred to the USCIS by the UNHCR. Again, however, only very few paths actually lead to resettlement. Even after refugee-status seekers are granted UNHCR referral, they must also be approved under the governing law of the host nation.[16] In short, an interview is not a guarantee of approval or admission.[17]

As a joined team, the State Department's PRM and the USCIS govern immensely critical influx affairs. With this duty comes the capacity to transform human potentiality; and life-affecting decisions are made on a daily basis. Each determination is significant and heralds its own dynamic range of long-term implications for intake individuals and nationalized citizens alike. The combined aim of these institutions is to facilitate a harmonious existence for all parties, without diminishing the safety, sanctity, or prosperity of its preexisting citizens.

In the event of approval, the individual or family will be aided in the processes of paperwork and processing. The agencies responsible for completing these aims are directly contracted through the U.S. government. Combined, they are referred to as Resettlement Support Centers (RSC). Next, the approved person or persons will be granted a loan for travel purposes. Travel is coordinated through the International Organization for Migration (IOM), contracted through the department of state.

Post-transition, a multitude of government and nongovernment organizations take over in aiding displaced asylum seekers as they enter the host country for the first time. In America, religious-based aid groups, such as Catholic Charities, Jewish Family Services, and Lutheran Family Services carry much of this weight. Schools, community centers, and private foundations also take on extraordinary caseloads.[18]

In fact, refugee-focused volunteer organizations, domestic and abroad, are central to the success of many third-party relocation efforts. These nonprofits often have a direct hand in the actual placement process, greeting and accommodating asylum seekers as they arrive in the new country. Such entities may also work to provide furniture, school clothes, parent literacy instruction, free translation services, school enrollment, job placement, medical advising, and drivers' license training.[19,20]

Digging Deeper: Paths to Resettlement

In considering possible outcomes for displaced persons, *voluntary repatriation* into the country of origin is always the primary objective.[21] In situations where this is not an immediate or long-term possibility, *localized resettlement* options will be considered. When this occurs, the temporary host country (typically the refugee camp sponsor of the displaced persons) will agree to absorb its refugee-status guests into its own country as free-moving individuals with national rights.

Localized resettlement (or local integration) countries are generally proximal to the zone of distress. Frequently, receiving countries are similarly affected by turmoil and instability, even while the circumstances of distress may differ. Therefore, it is not uncommon for nations in war-torn regions of the world to "flip-flop" their national citizens; as people leave one country to seek safety in another, others may be seeking haven from persecution in the reverse direction.

Third-party resettlement is the least desirable and least attempted solution. Only a miniscule fraction of the world's refugees will become eligible for relocation to a third-party host nation. A few make it through. They become our students.

HOME AWAY FROM HOME: SETTLING IN

Resettlement is work. It requires effort, strength, patience, tolerance, and forgiveness. It requires embracing, learning, growing, and renewing. Refugees and immigrants, in the very global sense, face the shared task of renovating and reconstructing every element of the former, pre-catastrophic life. Chaos produces disruption, trial, tragedy, confusion, and loss. In the longer term, gain and growth may also be evidenced. In any event, the likely end result is that new self-identities and fresh expectations will emerge.

An impressive number of relocated refugees and immigrants will eventually embrace the host domain with character and repute. These individuals will go on to work, attend universities, build professions, purchase homes, raise children, and contribute to their communities. Some will obtain citizenship and become fully acculturated, participating members of society. They become Americans.

Many Newcomers who resettle in the United States accomplish the aim with fervor, gusto, grace, and ultimately, success. Indeed, we are a country comprised of such individuals; we are a nation of incredibly diverse peoples, skills, assets, trades, and perspectives. This is an unparalleled and integral part of our international merit. This is the identical mantra of the Newcomer classrooms. We are the Ellis Islands of education.

SO, WHERE DOES THE FUNDING COME FROM?

What help (i.e., how much of taxpayer money) are Newcomer families entitled to? In the vast majority of resettlement cases, affected individuals receive only limited, provisional, and temporary financial or other resources. On this topic, the International Refugee Committee (IRC) writes:

> Many refugees come to the United States without any possessions and without knowing anyone. Other refugees come here to be reunited with family members. All refugees receive limited assistance from the U.S. government and non-profit organizations like the IRC.[22]

The United States, for instance, will provide initial haven transport for documented refugees. The commodity is received as a loan with an expected five-year repayment period. The government (or partnering nonprofit organization) will make provisional housing and job training/placement available. The receipt of this aid sets refugees apart from their immigrant peers, who do not receive any form of resettlement compensation or assistance from the U.S. government.

Funding for refugee and asylum initiatives is distributed through the U.S. Department of State. It is a part of a reserve held in the Migration and Refugee Assistance Account (MRA). The 2013 fiscal spending for refugees was $2.66 billion, and the emergency refugee assistance bank, called ERMA, maintains an annual cap of $100 million.[23]

While the United States has long maintained its role as the largest intake resource for refugees, its acceptance numbers are in certain decline, notably after the September 11 terrorist attacks. Nonetheless, the United States still accepts approximately the same number of refugees as all other hosting nations combined. Other key host nations include Australia, New Zealand, Canada, Norway, Sweden, and the Netherlands.[24]

FINAL THOUGHTS

Along the path to third-party resettlement, our prospective students and families will undergo an intrusive battery of tests. These mental, physical, and economic human analyses provide a framework for an individual's projected success in a given scenario (replacement, localized resettlement or long-distance relocation). Similar checks will determine foreign acceptance eligibility in countries such as England, Australia, France, and Switzerland.

Following final refugee-status approval, the IOM negotiates travel, and the travelers are assigned a voluntary organization that will oversee final travel and home placement arrangements. Several days, weeks, or months later, school office personnel arrive at our classroom door with new students. We are handed bus schedules and I.D. numbers, registered to impossible-to-pronounce names. If we're really lucky, we'll receive a barely decipherable prior scholastic record. Our job as greeter/teacher/ambassador/proctor/kid's jacket and shoe purchaser has only begun . . . again.

Ultimately, each reality—refugee or immigrant—is yoked to separate and unique sets of resettlement implications, which can, in turn, affect education and learning. In any case, it is prudent to keep in mind that all Newcomers are capable of full and complex contributions to our own Western societies. *Each* of our students and student guardians has something meaningful to contribute to the academic welfare of students, and also the community at large.

Some individuals are capable of gifting real-world advice about human circumstance on a global level. Others share academic knowledge or industry insight. Many provide critical trade, labor, and service skills. The vast majority of resettled refugees and immigrants *will* (and do!) make significant economic and civic contributions to the host country. If we are effective in our role as teachers, then we can also expect that our Newcomer students will grow to become positive, valued members of society.

In essence, all Newcomers hold the capacity to become the underwriters of language, history, community engagement, and heritage preservation; and this is at the very heart of the American spirit. *All* knowledge has a place. This is the main idea, the Big Picture, *the most important thing.*

Just for Fun!
Просто для удовольствия!—Russian
Famous Refugees

Josef Albers, Artist
Madeleine Albright (Czechoslovakia), Secretary of State
Hannah Arendt, Philosopher and Author

Bob Marley (Jamaica), Musician, Activist
Mikhail Baryshnikov(Russia), Dancer
Mebrahtom Keflezighi (Eritrea), Olympic Marathon Medalist
Max Beckmann, Artist
Luol Deng, Professional Basketball Player
Hans Bethe, Physicist and Nobel Laureate
Mario Stanic, Athlete
W. Michael Blumenthal, Sec of Treasury
M.I.A.(Sri Lanka), Recording Artist
Jackie Chan (Hong Kong), Actor, Athlete
Marc Chagall, Artist
Sonya Aho (Turkey), Journalist
Mahnza Afkhami (Iran), Women's Rights Activist, Writer
Bela Bartok (Hungary), Classical Composer
Miriam Makeba (South Africa), Singer
Andy Garcia (Cuba), Actor
Albert Chinualumogu Achebe (Nigeria), Writer
Luol Deng (Sudan), Basketball Player
Nadia Comaneci (Romania), Olympic Gymnast
Sigmund Freud (Austria), Psychology Pioneer
Salvador Dali, Artist
The Dalai Lama (Tibet), leader-in-exile, Nobel Laureate
Peter Drucker, Author, Management Consultant
Albert Einstein (Germany), Nobel Laureate
Marlene Dietrich (Germany), Actress
Wyclef Jean (Haiti), Recording Artist, Activist
Alek Wek (Sudan), Supermodel, Sudan
Max Ernst, Artist
Gloria Estefan, Singer
Lion Feuchtwanger, Author
K'Naan (Somalia), Rapper, Recording Artist
Alexander Ginsburg, Russian Cold War dissident
Roberto Goizuetta, former CEO of Coca Cola
Walter Gropius, Artist
George Grosz, Artist
Andrew S. Grove, Intel Corp., IRC Overseer
Henry Grunwald, Editor-in-Chief, Time Inc.,
Fabrice Muamba (Congo), Soccer Player, Bolton
John Heartfield, Artist
Thich Nhat Hanh, Zen Buddhist Master
Wassily Kandinsky, Artist
Henry Kissinger (Germany), Sec. of State, IRC Overseer

John Kemeny, Technology, Dartmouth Pres.
Sierra Leone Refugee All-Stars (Sierra Leone), Band
Andre Kertesz, Photographer
Oskar Kokoschka, Artist
Mika (Lebanon), Pop Musician
Namaa Alward (Iraq), Actress and Director
Madeleine Kunin, Swiss Ambassador, Gov. VT
Mebrahtom Keflezighi, Olympic Medalist
Lomana LuaLua, Athlete
Tom Lantos, U.S. Congressman (Calif)
Femand Leger, Artist
Jacques Lipchitz, Artist
Andre Masson, Artist
Mario Stanic (Sarajevo), Soccer Player, Chelsea
Andre Meyerhoff, Scientist and Nobel Laureate
Ludwig Mies van der Rohe, Architect
Dith Pran, Photographer
Gen. John Shalikashvili, Chairman-Joint Chiefs of Staff
Elie Wiesel (Romania), author, Nobel Laureate, IRC Overseer

Impressive, isn't it? What a testimony to the power of overcoming. Nepali and East Indian Hindu traditions share a commonly recited mantra: *Om Mani Padme Hum.* The verse roughly translates to: *the lotus blooms out of the mud.* That is, the lotus must push through layers of mud and silt, in order to find sunlight; and when the breakthrough finally occurs, its true beauty is revealed. *Om Mani Padme Hum* is the mantra for overcoming adversity. So it is with the human spirit—when positive intention, dedication, and perseverance are applied, miraculous things occur. This mantra encapsulates the energy and spirit of *our* Newcomer students.

NOTES

1. American Immigration Council (2013). Located at americanimmgrationcouncil.org. Retrieved Oct. 2012.

2. Russell, Sharon Stanton (2002). *Refugees: Risks and Challenges Worldwide.* Migration Policy Institute, 1946–4037.

3. Hamilton, Richards & Moore, Dennis (2004). Education of Refugee Children: Documenting and Implementing Change. In *Educational Interventions for Refugee Children*, eds Richard Hamilton & Dennis Moore, London UK: RoutledgeFalmer, Chapter 8.

4. McBrien, J. Lynn (2003). A Second Chance for Refugee Students. *Educational Leadership*, Vol. 61, No. 2, 76–9 O. *Educational Needs and Barriers for*

Refugee Students in the United States: A Review of Literature. Review of Educational Research Vol. 75, No. 3, 329–64.

5. United Nations, High Commissioner for Refugees (2012). *United Nations Communications and Public Information Service*, Geneva, Switzerland. Located at unhcr.org. Retrieved Aug. 2015.

6. McBrien, J. Lynn (2003). Educational Needs and Barriers for Refugee Students in the United States: A review of literature. *Review of Educational Research* Vol. 75. No. 3, 329–64

7. Patrick, Erin (2004). *The U.S. Refugee Resettlement Program.* Migration Policy Institute, Washington, D.C. Located at migrationpolicy.org/article/us-refugee-resettlement-program. Retrieved Aug. 2015.

8. United Nations Convention related to the Status of Refugees (1951). *UN Article 1.* Located at unhcr.org. Retrieved June 2011.

9. International Refugee Committee (2015). *SOAR*, New York, rescue.org, quoting United Nations Convention related to the Status of Refugees, Article 1., 1951. Retrieved Aug. 2015.

10. Van Hahn, Nguyen (2002). *Annual Report to Congress- Executive Summary.* Office of Refugee Resettlement. Located at acf.hhs.gov. Retrieved Dec. 2010.

11. Edwards, James R. Jr. (2012). *Religious Agencies and Refugee Resettlement.* Center for Immigration Studies. Memorandum, March 2012.

12. United Nations High Commissioner for Refugees (2012). *United Nations Communications and Public Information Service*, Geneva, Switzerland. Located at unhcr.org. Retrieved Aug. 2015.

13. U.S. Committee for Refugees & Immigrants (USCRI) (2015). Arlington, Va., refugees.org. Retrieved Aug. 2015.

14. U.S. Committee for Refugees & Immigrants (USCRI) (2015). Arlington, Va., refugees.org. Retrieved Aug. 2015.

15. United States Citizenship and Immigration Services (USCIS) (2013). *Path to Citizenship.* Located at uscis.gov. Retrieved Aug. 2015.

16. United Nations High Commissioner for Refugees (2012). United Nations Communications and Public Information Service, Geneva, Switzerland. Located at unhcr.org. Retrieved Aug. 2015.

17. U.S. Committee for Refugees & Immigrants (USCRI) (2015). Arlington, Va. Located at refugees.org. Retrieved Aug. 2015.

18. United States Citizenship and Immigration Services (USCIS) (2013). *Path to Citizenship.* Located at uscis.gov. Retrieved Aug. 2014.

19. International Refugee Committee (2015). *SOAR*, New York. Located at rescue. org. Retrieved Aug. 2015.

20. U.S. Committee for Refugees & Immigrants (USCRI) (2015). Arlington, Va. Located at refugees.org. Retrieved July 2013.

21. Patrick, Erin (2004). *The U.S. Refugee Resettlement Program.* Migration Policy Institute, Washington, D.C. Located at migrationpolicy.org/article/us-refugee-resettlement-program. Retrieved May. 2013.

22. International Refugee Committee (2015). *SOAR*, New York, rescue.org. Retrieved Aug. 2015.

23. United States Citizenship and Immigration Services (USCIS) (2013). *Path to Citizenship*. Located at uscis.gov. Retrieved Aug. 2015.

24. Russell, Sharon Stanton (2002). *Refugees: Risks and Challenges Worldwide.* Migration Policy Institute, 1946–4037.

Chapter 2

Defining the Newcomer Learner

qeexaya qofka ku cusub—Somali

TOWARD THE PRESENT: POLICY IN PLACE

As a nation, America has endured dramatic swings of sentiment—and much has changed since the country's first days—regarding the relationship between host and heritage languages of its peoples. These tides of ideal and expectation have resulted in dramatic discrepancies in language policy.

In the late seventeenth century, the infant city of Manhattan embraced some twenty daily exchange languages, outside of the multitude of Native American tongues spoken throughout the region.[1] In this era, the ability to speak more than one language proved a definitive asset. Multilingualism was also a key endowment for social-status maneuverability.

To the same extent, immigrants maintained great pride in their native language, culture, and customs. Many exercised fantastic liberties to preserve these heritage qualities in the new nation. Entire schools, workplaces, churches, gathering halls, and communities were established with the specific aim of cultural proliferation; and many groups thrived because of it.[2]

A new and notably immense multitude of immigrants made their way to America in the early nineteenth century. The vast majority of these settlement pioneers came from Europe. More than five million originated from Germany alone.[3]

A number of linguistic-heritage facets demonstrated strong presence. Among these, German, Dutch, Polish, Italian, French, Norwegian, Czech, Swedish, Spanish, and Danish were the strongest contenders. Remarkably, America did not claim any unified national language, at least for the purposes

17

of education, for the duration of the nineteenth century. Most children were educated in bilingual or trilingual contexts, most commonly in Spanish, German, and French.

Eventually, the issue of a prevailing uniform language in Americanized schooling did surface as a major issue in policy reform. Language policy debates were rarely centered on the facilitation of a learner's emotional or social well-being. Instead, they found root in logistical straightforwardness and instantaneous productivity. Consequently, leaders of the new educational reform were disinclined to preserve or perpetuate dual-language-learning programs. Only at this time did "ethnic politics" appear on the scene as a driving force in our nation's early dual-language instructional policies.[4]

Educational and language reform intensified during the 1880s and 1890s. This period ushered in a dramatic social push for nationalism; and new instructional protocol reflected this. The idling notion of a unified national identity gained incredible momentum. Before long, word of America's desperate search to define, categorize, and label its own inherent composite resulted in a new national reputation. This, in time, evolved into a more recognizable neo-American identity.

Faced with the looming crossover into the twentieth century, America sensed and responded to the influence of increasing global distress. This brooding tension would eventually manifest as the First World War. With these new developments, nationalism assumed a star presence on America's political stage.

From this, the quest for *oneness*—that is, complete unification—became paramount. Under the umbrella of nationalism, cohesiveness became an undeniable asset, at least in terms of national gain and prosperity. Ultimately, unification idealism bore immediate educational implications, leading to measures to promote standardization in policy and practice.

Almost overnight, language adherence was converted to a high-scale issue. English language fluency became an instantaneous and finite indicator of nationalistic loyalty. Moreover, many policy makers were inspired by the idea that strict devotion to a unified national language could bring solidarity swiftly to the nation in a time of great uncertainty. In short order, English was proclaimed the official language of the United States of America.

The year 1906 ushered in additional English language legislation, known as the Naturalization Act. The new law mandated that any immigrant wishing to become a naturalized U.S. citizen must first prove his or her ability to demonstrate English proficiency. The Naturalization Act was paramount in determining a set course for the next century of language use, as well as language instruction, in the United States.

Not surprisingly, the policy makers of this generation recognized that only one demographic, the youth, could enact real linguistic change. So began the prodigious effort to Americanize all citizens. Academia in the United States was reborn as the essential foundation for this aim.

Speaking well ahead of his time, nineteenth-century school superintendent William Torrey Harris brilliantly captured realities of an educational duplicity that continue to confound modern generations. He proposed that "[true] . . . schools must 'Americanize' language minority children. [Yet] national memories and aspirations, family traditions, customs and habits, moral and religious observances cannot suddenly be removed or changed without disastrously weakening the personality."[5,6]

The resurgence of nationalism during the World War eras resulted in rehabilitated initiatives to capture language solidarity, among other things. With the nation's preindustrial model shift, the template for instruction, too, inherited a mechanical nature. Thus, the factory-school model was born and subsequently thrived.

As a result, students enrolled in formal U.S. schooling, specifically English Language Learners (ELLs), experienced a very different academic reality than their scholastic predecessors. With regard to language instruction, English structure and grammar were emphasized. Meanwhile, the push for oral proficiency also gained momentum.

The chief branches of instructional protocol included rote memorization, recall, word-centric mimicry, and drill procedures—all ear tags of the *grammar-translation method*. Grammar-translation maintained a certain stronghold into the 1950s, though new theories were already advertising impetus for change. New approaches to English Language Acquisition (ELA) instruction allowed for preliminary psychological and behaviorism considerations. New models often reflected Skinner's stimuli-response-reward strategy. The combined language instruction techniques of the 1950s comprise the *audio-lingual method*.

The sixties and seventies saw a resurgence of interest and theory in the field of ELA education. Dozens of revolutionary English language instructional models were proposed, introduced, and implemented in this pedagogical generation, including Curan's *Community Language Learning* and Krashen's *Natural Approach* (silent-allowance learning). Many of these freshly articulated templates for English acquisition were experimental and short-lived; others maintain their value—and are even practiced with fidelity—in modern classrooms.

America in the 1980s oversaw a dramatic 38 percent rise in speakers of other languages (SOLs). This trend, according to the 2000 Census reports, continued into the 1990s, with a 47 percent increase. The refugee and immigrant influx of the 1980s and 1990s deeply affected public perception regarding ELLs. Overall, sentiments surrounding SOLs became less positive, and support for heritage culture and language in the mainstream diminished.

Pronounced changes in the immigration dynamic prompted certain feelings of anxiety, frustration, or fear among host citizens. A new sentiment was brewing. Many Americans were beginning to "fear that English, the language that has taken over the globe, is actually in danger at home."[7] English-threat paranoia boomed in the years from 1980, influencing virtually every aspect of present-day language use and restriction policy.[8]

The reality, of course, is that SOLs could not possibly derail the fortitude of English as America's primary language. Nor could they demonstrate the singular power to fracture the inherent integrity of our nation. To a further extent, multiple researchers set out to prove the complete opposite—that is, Newcomers and ELLs overwhelmingly *lend* to our national greatness, rather than detract from it.

To begin, SOLs may demonstrate more host language capacity than we are likely to give them credit for. Brown provides the statistics on this issue, speaking in the context of the refugee and immigrant influx of the 1980s and 1990s.

> Of the 47 million minority-language speakers over five years old now in the country, 43.6 million of them speak at least some English, and over half of them speak English fluently. With time, the rest will achieve fluency or something close to it. And their descendants will likely become monolingual English speakers.[9]

In slow measure, the actual utility of native language communication achieved recognition, even within second language social and instructional utilities. In the late 1990s, a limited number of schools and districts pronounced official tolerance for SOLs in public education settings. This cleared the path for future acceptance of bilingualism as a legitimate mechanism for speaking, learning, and interacting with others in the host classroom setting.

In recent years, the bilingualism trend has evolved dramatically, with special regard for Spanish-speaking ELLs. Encouraged bilingual acceptance in Spanish (ELA-Spanish) spilled over into teaching and learning protocol for all other ELLs (ELA-English). Across the nation, new programs were created to actually *encourage* bilingual learning. While bilingual models were—and continue to be—contested best practices, they do occur in our modern schools, often with terrific learning success rates. Ironically, by the 2010s, bilingual study also became concomitant with prestige and privilege. Currently, private and public international schools are demanding high status on the educational stage.

The early stages of ELA-E education in America have permeated our current ELA instruction era and deeply influence our present-day practices. Still, we have covered incredible distances since the era of native language rejection; and many dimensions of language-learning pedagogy have been reworked, even in the last decades. Fresh ideas and approaches continue to emerge and find their way into our most effective learning environments.

As we become more experienced practitioners of the Newcomer education craft, we also become key contributors to an ever-growing ocean of tools, tips, tricks, approaches, and ideas. We are again redefining ELA education for ourselves. And we're not afraid to get in the mud.

Ultimately, our American DNA remains intact. That is, we are still a geographically bound kaleidoscope of cultural, linguistic, genetic, and artistic factors, interwoven with remarkable intricacies and layers of personal, familial, social, and civic depth. Our task now lies in merging these tremendous attributes in a singular classroom setting, in order to bring out our students' highest socio-academic capabilities. We are the continual authors of this unique Newcomer education story. We draft new pages in each classroom day.

GLOBAL CLASSROOMS: NEWCOMERS IN THE HOST SCHOOL SYSTEM

Policy regarding the educational placement for Newcomers, including access to language-learning services, was redesigned in the early twentieth century. Under current laws, children who enter the United States for the first time must register for and participate in state-approved education programs alongside their American counterparts. Students who are also ELLs have additional legal options available to them that can affect the language education services that they are provided.

First, a student must be classified as an ELL in order to be considered eligible for the full spectrum of related ELA services. It is the primary obligation of a learning institution to responsibly qualify or classify ELLs according to an array of measurable and nonmeasurable factors.

In many cases, refugee and immigrant families who are resettled through a third-party agency are aided in the school enrollment processes by the facilitating organization. Translators, where available, may accompany family members and case workers to a school. Case workers, meanwhile, are trained to aid parents in requesting ELA considerations for their child at the time of enrollment.

Any student whose primary home language is not English will be pre-screened for language proficiency, via any number of standardized literacy, writing, listening, and/or oral formats before they are officially assigned to a classroom(s). The most relevant assessments are state and/or nationally coordinated assessments. In the school setting, the acronyms CELA, ACCESS for ELLs, CELDT, iTEP, and STAR are associated with language ability testing.

If a student does not meet the provisions for Early Advanced or Advanced English language capabilities, the student will be defined as an ELL. Subsequently, the child will qualify for provisional services and accommodations in this arena. Also, under current statutes, if a child is more than two years below grade level and is also eligible for testing accommodations on the basis of language, he or she is eligible for ELA-E programming.

ELLs who *do* achieve proficiency on Assessing Comprehension and Communication in English State-to-State (ACCESS) or similar tests are to be considered for mainstream status, with appropriate supports in place. Determinations to exit a student from ELA programming are reliant upon a full body of evidence. Such evidence may include: test measures, teacher and parental input, psychological and behavioral data, annotated WIDA "can do" indicators (WIDA is no longer used as an acronym; it is a widely used English language standardized testing tool), and student work samples.

Once an ELA-E/ELA-S designated child has been placed on our roster, the charge of adhering to all legal mandates becomes integral to our role as professional educators. We are typically aided in this task by the school assessment leader (SAL) or other administrative personnel, whose focus is to ensure school-wide accountability. Qualifying legal classroom measures might include individualized education program (IEP) and/or individual learning plan (ILP) fulfillment; routine ELA intervention access; student growth documentation; and state-mandated plans and tests. The current learning generation is primarily assessed by the Partnership for Assessment of Readiness for College and Careers (PARCC).

A bit overwhelming, isn't it? So let's back up. Once an ELA-E/ELA-S designated child has been placed on our roster, the charge of adhering to smiles, hugs, safety, structure, exploration and learning fun becomes our teacher responsibility. The rest will come together. I promise.

NOTES

1. Crawford, James (1992). *Language Loyalties, Historical Roots of U.S. Language Policy.* University of Chicago Press, Chicago.

2. Cambourne, Brian (1995). Toward an Educationally Relevant Theory of Literacy Learning: Twenty Years of Inquiry. *The Reading Teacher*, Vol. 49, No. 3.

3. Crawford, James (1992). *Language Loyalties, Historical Roots of U.S. Language Policy.* University of Chicago Press, Chicago.

4. Cambourne, Brian (1995). Toward an Educationally Relevant Theory of Literacy Learning: Twenty Years of Inquiry. *The Reading Teacher*, Vol. 49, No. 3.

5. Cambourne, Brian (1995). Toward an Educationally Relevant Theory of Literacy Learning: Twenty Years of Inquiry. *The Reading Teacher*, Vol. 49, No. 3.

6. Crawford, James (1992). *Language Loyalties, Historical Roots of U.S. Language Policy.* University of Chicago Press, Chicago.

7. Baron, Dennis (2011). *English Spoken Here? What the 2000 Census Tells Us About the USA.* Located at english.illinois.edu. Retrieved Aug. 2011.

8. Tse, Lucy (2001). *Why Don't they Learn English? Separating Fact from Fallacy in the U.S. Language Debate.* New York Teachers College Press.

9. Brown, Douglas H. (2006). *Principals of Language Learning and Teaching* (5th Edition). Pearson Education ESL.

Chapter 3

Culture Shock and Social Adjustment

Культурны шок і сацыяльнай адаптацыі-Belarusian

TRANSITION, TRAUMA AND LEARNING

Most resettled refugees and immigrants have endured trauma. These pains are rarely documented or officially diagnosed, and are often only shared in the arena of private, trusted conversation, if at all. With regard to our resettled Newcomer learners, there is a terrific potential for underpinning mental and behavioral intricacies to surface in the classroom setting.

Post-resettlement refugees are disproportionately vulnerable to mental distress. This fact presents exceptional and uncomfortable challenges for our Newcomer students. In fact, any aspect of refugee plight "places refugee children and young people potentially at risk of developing learning difficulties, behavioral problems and psychological distress . . . [resulting in] less than optimal outcomes at school."[1,2]

Stressful life events, including moving or school relocation, can affect mental health and induce behavior-related changes in children. Physical transition can result in diminished control and loss of familiar guideposts, especially when the change is unanticipated. If and when abrupt transition threatens to overwhelm an individual's accessible coping resources, then mental functioning can be compromised.[3]

Our students demonstrate an array of stress indicators, many of which are nonverbal. These include irritability, sleepiness, restlessness, aggression, withdrawn personality, bedwetting, concentration difficulties, diminished school performance, hoarding, and high-risk behavior. Stress-induced tendencies can manifest in any individual, and are not limited by age, gender, race, or circumstance.[4–6]

The *degree* to which our Newcomer students are impacted by stress can be notably profound. We can assume that most Newcomers will have endured episodes of prolonged stress, as an organic byproduct of abrupt flight. Of course, affectedness presents itself in individualized ways, and it is intensely codependent upon the length and gradation of stressful experience, as well as a string of alternative variables.

For example, age at the time of traumatic encounter can influence the extent and degree of symptomatic stress behavior. The two critical periods of vulnerability in the young refugee's life are preschool and early adolescence.[7] Both are imperative stages in human development, especially in terms of identity sculpting and enriching one's sense-making capacities.[8] Refugee

Table 3.1 Risk Factors

Imbedded Conditional Risk Factors	Pre-Migration Risk Factors	Post-resettlement/Ongoing Risk Factors
• Poverty	• Persecution	• Degree of culture shock
• Malnutrition	• Famine	• View of stress and coping
• Low-birth weight	• War	• New housing adjustments
• Early birth	• Violence	• Language proficiency level
• Perinatal complications	• Flight	• Degree of previous school experiences
• Perinatal and infant toxicity exposure	• Loss of stability	• Financial sustainability
• Family stability	• Loss of loved ones and pets	• Level of cultural expectation alignment
• Internal locus of control	• Loss of property	• Accessibility to heritage culture communities and support groups
• Academic access and perceived success	• Insufficient medical care	• Available resettlement resources in the host society
• History of abuse	• Previous history or exposure to trauma	• Attitudes about host and home countries
• History of disease	• Positive or negative perception of host country	• Teacher awareness and efficacy in working with ELLs
• History of distress	• Experienced discrimination	• Employment factors in the host society
• Death of loved ones	• Family dis-cohesion and dysfunction	
• Loss of or separation from parent	• Parental inadequacies	

children who are relocated during these two age categories are at a heightened risk for traumatic scarring, adjustment complications, and academic challenges.[9]

Family cohesiveness, exposure to violence, and physical distance of geographic relocation are other important considerations. The potential set of risk factors that can influence stress susceptibility is far-reaching. Certain refugee and Newcomer stress risk behaviors commonly present themselves in the classroom setting. They are highlighted below.

TRAUMATIC STRESS AND THE REFUGEE STUDENT

Newcomer children may not show any immediate symptoms of post-traumatic stress. Nonetheless, any individual who has been exposed to pre-resettlement violence and upheaval may be considered *at risk* for experiencing short- or long-term mental and emotional consequences of forced flight.[10] Stressors related to the refugee experience prompt aggravated internal responses, which may exceed reactive norms, and consequently overwhelm an individual's emotional, social, and cognitive capacities. As self-ownership and sense-making capabilities are diminished, post-traumatic stress can occur.

Many children and their parents will suffer from some degree of Post-Traumatic Stress Syndrome. PTSS is a disabling life condition with the capacity to devastate an individual's ability to participate in everyday life in normal functioning ways. Not all Newcomers are at risk of developing PTSS; many may never even show signs of its milder psychological cousins. Still, the potential—and probability—of affectedness are very real. An estimated 45%–60% of children who have traumatic experiences will also develop corresponding post-traumatic stress disorders.[11]

Traumatic reactions can mimic transition stress symptoms, but may be significantly more frequent and/or more pronounced. They might include depression, anxiety, survivor's remorse, vulnerability, and subjection. Severe loss and/or distress can manifest in somatic forms, including headaches, eczema, upset stomach, sleeplessness, clinginess, temper-tantrums, distractedness, fantasy play, and learning difficulties. Specific somatic symptoms regularly cluster around a particular group or groups, and may hint at inherent underlying cultural beliefs and tendencies.[12,13]

In the classroom setting, we look for PTSS symptoms as they are manifested in four distinct areas: affective, physical, cognitive, and behavioral.[14, 15] *Affective* traits include depression, anxiety, guilt, anger, detachment, and pessimism. Headaches, fatigue, sleep apnea, night sweats, nightmares, nausea, sensory sensitivities, and heightened defense mechanisms are all *physical* manifestations of PTSS.

Cognitive attributes incorporate disinterest, self-blame, memory and concentration deficits, recurring trauma, numbness, a negative self-view, and suicidal thoughts. Meanwhile, regressive patterns, such as clinginess, withdrawal, repetitive play, self-talk, isolation, agitation, delinquency, and aggression are common *behavioral* outcomes of post-traumatic stress.

When we are able to notice, name, and understand a particular student behavior, we are more likely to correctly prescribe and enact reactive plans for short- and long-term learner success. Perhaps a student is unable to concentrate in class, has very low self-esteem, and demonstrates a need for constant physical touch. We might consequently recognize the potentiality for cognitive affect.

Therefore, we can provide kinesthetic tools to stimulate tactile responses. We might also seek out definitive strengths that we can highlight. Students might also be encouraged to share their expertise in very small, nurturing team settings.

affective:

DEPRESSION, ANXIETY, GUILT, ANGER, DETACHMENT, GRIEF, PESSIMISM

physical:

HEADACHES, FATIGUE, SLEEP APNEA, NIGHTMARES, SWEATS, HEIGHTENED SENSORY AND DEFENSE MECHANISMS

traumatic stress indicators

cognitive:

RE-EXPERIENCE OF TRAUMA, SELF-BLAME, LOSS OF INTEREST, MEMORY AND CONCETRATION DEFICITS, NUMBNESS, NEGATIVE PERCEPTIONS, SUICIDAL THOUGHTS.

behavioral:

REGRESSIVE PATTERNS– WITHDRAWL, REPETITIVE PLAY, SELF-TALK, CLINGINESS, ISOLATION, AGITATION, EDGINESS, AGGRESSION, DELIQUENCY

Figure 3.2   **Stress Indicators**

We are teachers. Most of us are not authorities on psychological distress; nor would we ever claim to be. Still, it cannot hurt us to be informed. In fact, an improved awareness of our students' *whole* picture can only serve to increase our efficacy as educators and empower our students as learners. It is worth our effort and understanding. Our students deserve it.

SHOCK IN THE CLASSROOM CONTEXT

Transition shock is a very real phenomenon. Transition shock is an overarching umbrella for risk factors related to disorientation and compromised frames of reference that can occur as a result of relocation. Transitional traumas are associated with abrupt disconnects, such as those that typify refugee and immigrant resettlement patterns. These types of traumas include culture shock, PTSS, and erratic assimilation behaviors.[16]

Culture Shock

Culture shock is elicited via exposure to social, physical, or cultural elements that are perceived by an individual to be unfamiliar, unsafe, or unpredictable. Our Newcomer students will have endured any degree of forced disengagement from known elements, such as heritage language, customs, geographical guideposts, and family and religious support systems. As a domino effect, personal ideals, morals, value sets, and life goals may also be called into question, as self-beliefs are pinned against the existing social fabric of the host culture. This process of intense intra-assessment and heritage/host appraisal can wreak havoc on an individual's self-esteem, and may underwrite subsequent self-identity dilemmas.[17,18]

Culture shock can manifest from a variety of causes across a broad platform of stages, and it may be agitated by any number of potential triggers. Individual manifestations of culture shock may vary according to age, self-preparedness, and degree of prior exposure. Symptoms can range from mild annoyance to paralyzing disturbance.

Best practices encourage us to consider the whole child. In doing so, we look for specific cues in our learners that signal the presence of culture shock. Nearly all Newcomer students demonstrate elements of culture shock, without mind to immigrant, refugee, geographical, or financial background. The key is in identifying approximately *where* on the spectrum our students currently reside, as well as what progress we'd like them to achieve throughout the school year and beyond.

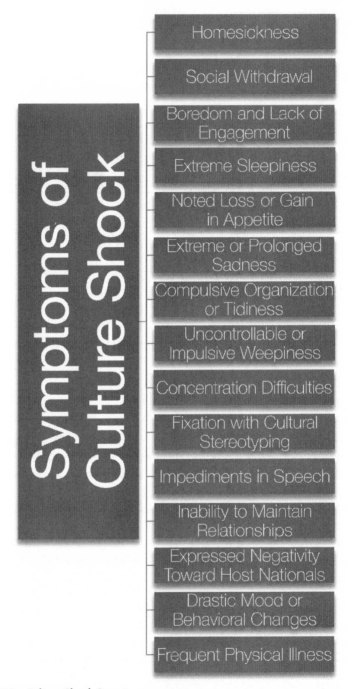

Figure 3.3   Culture Shock Symptoms

4 Corners: The Domains of Culture Shock

Shock may be characterized as *individualized manifestations of the human experience at a particular time, under a given set of circumstances.* Like other adjustment cycles that are intertwined with bereavement, cultural shock follows a predictable healing process. We refer to these domains as the honeymoon, negotiation, adjustment, and mastery phases. Each phase has specific implications for brain development and learning, all with the potential to influence our Newcomer students.[19]

Domains of Culture Shock

1. Honeymoon: Cultural differences are viewed in a romanticized light; this is a period of intense intake, awe, and discovery. Shock and fascination may delay stress sensors.
2. Negotiation: Internal struggles with cultural differences manifest as frustration, anxiety, fear, detachment, physical discomfort, and homesickness. (~3 months)
3. Adjustment: Period of acceptance, sense making, maneuverability, and measurable efficacy in the new environment. Anxiety and dysfunction are significantly reduced. (~6–12 months)
4. Mastery: (Bicultural stage). Here, individuals are able to navigate freely and successfully in the new culture; self-efficiency is maintained. (~1–5 years)

A Closer Look: Adjustment Domain

Each of the culture shock domains presents separate and extensive implications for every influenced individual. For our purposes as educators, we will develop our understanding of the adjustment domain. The three compartments of the adjustment domain are *Isolation, Adoption, and Integration.*[20] Most Newcomers adhere to one of these profiles in its near entirety, and outcomes of each separate phase show up differently in the classroom. Figure 3.4 illustrates the specific domain highlights.

A separate, but remarkably aligned adjustment rubric was published in 1974 by cross-cultural psychologist John W. Barry. Barry's acculturation theory holds that transitioning individuals will pass through any of four adjustment quadrants, which he names: *Marginalization, Separation* (or *Preservation,* according to Schumman), *Assimilation,* and *Integration.*[21]

Separation/Preservation requires that heritage, cultural, and language value systems are upheld exclusively, at the utter expense of host country participation. In effect, all aspects of the host culture are rejected. This quadrant mirrors isolation. *Assimilation,* conversely, reflects the concept of adoption. It denotes full espousal of the new culture and language, but is void of efforts to maintain or nurture heritage custom and language.

isolation Isolation is marked by disengagement with host culture. The individual may view the host environment as harsh, unwelcoming, or disinviting. He or she is likely to experience conflict with host culture principles on a range of functional, physical, linguistic, moral, or religious platforms.

Isolated persons are highly likely to return to the origination country. However, they may experience additional conflict and/or misalliance in returning to the native country or customs. They might also be experience difficulty relating to culturally similar groups or individuals in the host setting, should they choose to remain. Thus, isolated individuals find themselves apart and detached from both heritage and host alliances.

adoption Adoption is signaled by utter identification with the new culture at the expense of the heritage identity. Individuals who wholly adopt the new culture are highly likely to remain in the host nation without return to pre-resettlement area. It is expected that these persons will experience a loss of home language, customs, and loyalty, for themselves and for future generations.

When cultural adoption takes place, full rejection of the home culture, customs, dress, or language can occur. Social isolation, at least with regard to family and heritage culture support groups, is also common. Those who experience cultural adoption may feel as though they are on the "outside" of the both home and host dynamics.

integration Integrated individuals have relocate successfully. These persons manage to recognize positive attributes of both the home and host cultures, and can navigate each with relative ease. Integration refers to the full, healthy assimilation into the new culture without the loss or the old.

One sign of integration is a developed understanding of societal nuances, both overt and underlying. Integrated individuals are likely to experience well-being and a sense of overarching social acceptance. Self-efficacy, cooperative human connectivity, and general productivity are probable outcomes.

Figure 3.4   Isolation/Adoption

Marginalization, meanwhile, is a stagnant growth state in which both the heritage and the host cultures are rejected. Neither culture is embraced; and thus, neither has grounding value. Marginalized individuals may identify as "floaters" in the overarching social framework. This is the least desirable quadrant, as it is almost entirely deficient of belongingness.

Finally, *Integration* embodies a healthy marriage between heritage and host cultures. Our Newcomer students and their family members will fall somewhere on this spectrum of acculturation. Ultimately, integration is optimal. In this way, pre-transition identities are preserved, even as new social adaptations are underway. Positive and negative virtues of *both* the home and host cultures may be processed somewhat objectively, and a reasonable "meeting in the middle" is achieved.

SOCIAL MOBILITY AND ASSIMILATION

Let's imagine that we have just relocated into a novel environment and are operating out of will, trepidation, and uncertainty. In the interim moments of sanity, we must decipher how to manipulate our new stove and refrigerator; how to maneuver around the westernized toilet; how to board a public bus and seek out our child's projected school or how to explain in non-Burmese that the elder son has seizures and requires special attention. Oh, and then, there's that challenge about getting a job and providing for our family.

Complex social adjustment needs such as these lie just beyond the perimeters of basic physical needs. These intrapersonal prerequisites also itch to be satisfied, perhaps on a competing level with the physical components of human fulfillment. Specifically, Newcomer individuals, across all platforms are faced with one essential conundrum: *How do I fit in?*

Many are able to manage a solution to this dilemma. Some don't. Others find themselves somewhere in the middle; floating, but without foundation. As a mark of forced migration, Newcomers often experience intense conflicts between their heritage and assimilative cultural roles, resulting in awkward cultural duplicity. In other words, many find themselves with one foot steeped in tradition, while another limb grasps for a stronghold in the new sociodynamic. Unfortunately, the grounds for transition are rarely sturdy; and grace is elusive when teetering along the line of a fence.

Newcomers who are able to achieve integration are also likely to experience upward mobility, which occurs when the individual achieves a high standard of inter- and intrapersonal comfort and fluid maneuverability in the host setting. A large majority of immigrants (and a disproportionately small number of refugees) fall into this category.[22]

When only partial or limited integration are realized, Newcomers are predicted to fall into one of two less desirable categories. The first of these, *upward mobility plus ethnic solidarity* applies when upward mobility has been partially experienced, but is also coupled with fierce loyalty and clinging to the home culture at the expense of the host culture. Individuals in this category will function with notable efficacy in the new environment, but may reject "fitting in" to the new society. Again, immigrants are more likely to inhabit this domain than their refugee-relocated counterparts.

Some individuals *will* make the physical transition to the host country, but will also encounter exceptional challenges or hesitations related to the assimilation process. In this case, the outcome is one of *downward mobility*. Unfortunately, the downward mobility bracket serves as a broad sweeping

- Successful integration into middle-class white majority
- Ability to work and comfortably support immediate family
- Achievement of literary, oral, and normative behavior fluency
- High majority of voluntary immigrants; thin proportion of refugee population

- Medium upward mobility, with successful integration at some levels
- Strong cultural community ties exist, sometimes at the expense of host culture attachment or receptivity
- High majority of voluntary and non-voluntary immigrants and certain refugee factions (Irish, Cuban Vietnamese)

- Minimal or unobservable upward mobility
- Assimilation into poverty, inner-city habitation, underclass designation
- Cultural dissonance as young people move away from parents and culture
- Unhealthy social groups may form
- Crime and unemployment may be high and unavoidable

Downward mobility typically follows:
- A pronounced majority of resettled refugees
- Marginal numbers of involuntary migrants
- A small percentage of voluntary migrants

Figure 3.5   Mobility Map

net for a multitude of ELL families who assimilate into poverty. This is not surprising, considering that the vast majority of refugee-sanctioned Newcomers are resettled into government project housing, with scarce accessibility to resources that promote forward economic capacity.

Downward mobility may increase the likelihood for unemployment, crime, and a tendency to belong to unhealthy social factions, such as gangs. It may also spur dissonance, wherein individuals become detached and resistant, or project defiance toward the home culture. Younger generations may turn away from their traditional families, seeking out new sets of relatives who are more closely aligned with presumed social norms.[23]

Children may reject heritage indicators, such as language, dress, cultural celebration, and religion. As a result, healthy home structures, key indicators for upward mobility, can become damaged or altogether depleted. Downward mobility affects refugee populations in the greatest numbers, followed by involuntary immigrant groups, and finally, voluntary immigrants.[24]

LOCUS IS NOT AN INSECT: THE GRIEF CYCLE AND INTERNAL LOCUS OF CONTROL

Throughout recorded history, humans have attempted to analyze, dissect, and make sense of grief. This is our nature: we want to know, to grasp, to get to the bottom of things, and to have a final say. In all these millennia of experiential interrogation, the best we can do is to seek out a *probable* pattern of grieving events. Neimeyer (1988) subdivides grieving into three fundamental stages of extreme, unanticipated loss: avoidance, assimilation, and accommodation.[25]

Avoidance is hallmarked by initial confusion, shock, disorientation, and panic. From this state, it is impossible to comprehend the true nature of the ordeal, and grief cannot be purposefully addressed. Many incoming Newcomers will still be in this initial phase when they enter resettlement classrooms.

Assimilation occurs after the initial period of shock, when the grief-affected person is able to digest certain aspects of the trauma. Intense feelings and depression are common outcomes of assimilation, and are demonstrated through sadness, despair, isolation, loneliness, sleepiness, sleeplessness, changes in appetite, and psychological down-talk.[26,27]

Accommodation is the final phase in the grief cycle. In this period, the individual comes into an acceptance of the trauma or loss. Emotions become less debilitating. As the person regains his or her footing, the process of moving forward can begin. Interestingly, an individual who has passed through these stages as the result of severe traumatic upset or transition is said to have added an entire additional phase onto the typical human life cycle.[28]

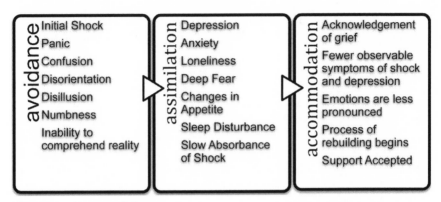

Figure 3.6   Accommodations

We can make the most profound impact when we are also willing to be cognizant of at least some of what occurs beneath the surface of our students. It may be easier for us to discover patience for our learners when we take into account any number of potential obstructions that may be present. Also, we may uncover patience for ourselves, as we understand that our chosen alcove of the educational practice is *all about wait time*. Fortunately, the rewards for our calm fortitude are so exceptionally worth any delayed results!

COPING MECHANISMS

Coping mechanisms are an essential element of humanity. These conscious and unconscious reactions to stress enable an individual to regain normative values of the ego and its physical environs. Coping mechanisms, in their innate and unembellished state, are healthy and advantageous behaviors. Child survivor refugees will demonstrate any number of coping mechanisms in the classroom setting. They are most frequently evidenced through *denying, silencing, avoiding, and minimizing past or current experiences.*

Interestingly, children and adults employ these measures in an effort to protect the self as well as the generational counterpart. For example, adults model coping strategies for their children, deliberately or subliminally, and with sheltering intent. Children often carry out similar efforts to shield the parents from perceived discomfort.

The latter episode is frequently played out in the post-resettlement scenario. In this context, children may have the opportunity to digest more of the host-culture language and social nuances than their elders. Consequently, they may internalize a responsibility to protect and help parents navigate the new territory.

Best practices in education call for us to embrace and teach to the whole child. That includes working with, through, and *because of* coping tendencies.

Don't be afraid to pull these survival mechanisms out of the dark. Relish them. Appreciate them. Then, guide students in letting them go.

The Silent Period and Obstructed Speech

The effects of a child's emotional and psychiatric distress are routinely fleshed out in the Newcomer classroom. Often, the first of these symptoms are speech related. In many cases, newly resettled students endure a period of marked silence. Silence is usually ascribed to the process of emotional transitioning. During the silent phase, which lasts for variant lengths of time, an individual will not express thoughts in the host language, either out of reluctance or inability.[29] Those who experience this phenomenon are sometimes referred to as "shell shocked."[30,31] The silent phase can last a period of days, weeks, or months.

In addition to silence, exposure to traumatic episodes at any period in a child's life can trigger recurring nightmares and cognitive delays, as well as speech "freezes" and impediments. Such blocks include stuttering. Newcomer students who exhibit impeded speech should also be evaluated for traumatic stress.

Both silence and stuttering have a need to be addressed in the classroom. To begin, students should not be expected or mandated to produce oral language before they are ready. It is also wise to avoid situations that might embarrass new language learners, including publicly calling on them to speak before they are ready. We can be careful to offer caring encouragement and guidance. Also, we are responsible to practice patient wait time for processing speakers. In doing so, we model this behavior for other students.

Specific classroom accommodations must be in place to support language learners, and particularly nonverbal ELLs. First, to achieve this, a healthy and nurturing learning environment is critical. Small group engagement, tactile activities, and positive feedback may encourage speech attempts and decrease overall anxiety. Alternative-expression tasks, such as drawing-and-labeling, script singing, or charade acting can provide additional opportunities to demonstrate knowledge in a language-centric environment.

Of course, kindness and caring are often the most influential antidotes to stress-stemmed silence. In the context of nonverbal ELLs, relationship and safety are everything. Simply, security induces speech.

Re-presentation

Students with refugee and/or migratory backgrounds are highly likely to relive, or experience re-presentation of past traumatic events on a recurrent basis.[32] In the classroom, re-presentation may be played out in a student's efforts to recreate various aspects of the disturbance. These behaviors are frequently observed through drawing, writing, play-acting, or repeated retelling of the event. Re-presentation can also occur through intrusive dreaming, which can negatively interfere with a child's normal sleep cycle, and lack of sleep, in turn, can impact a student's school performance.

Survivor's Guilt

Survivor's guilt is a term used to describe intense feelings of guilt or shame that can manifest in the aftermath of leaving loved ones behind. Survivor's guilt is prolific among relocated refugee and immigrant populations.[33] An affected individual may be burdened by notions of abandoning pre-resettlement entities or causing harm to others through the act of leaving. Many will feel undeserving of, or ill-equipped for, new opportunities in the host setting.

Guilt, shame, embarrassment, and worthlessness are toxic properties, and they can debilitate an individual's functional capacities to a partial or full extent. Feelings of intense guilt and shame can become exacerbated by various stimuli along the path to recovery. Not surprisingly, they can also impact integration and learning in potentially negative ways.

Parents may feel guilt for not being able to provide basic needs, including safety and stability, for their own family and for those left behind. Children can feel the weight of not saying goodbye to loved ones, pets, or friends, and may feel guilt in not being able to properly serve parents in their new-found roles as translators, bill payers, and social mediators. In any event, survivor's guilt deserves acknowledgment and therapeutic treatment, whenever possible; the weight of its presence can be a debilitating factor in post-resettlement adjustment.[34]

Guilt and shame add several layers of challenge (and opportunity) within our Newcomer classrooms. Our objective is to listen, guide, and aid in the healing process, where we are able. We need to be mindful that guilt and shame can influence cognitive functioning; and we can model patience, self-love, and acceptance.

School Performance Stress

The pressure to perform well academically can contribute to a heightened level of learner stress. Newcomers and refugees may be especially vulnerable to pressure to excel in school. This is due, in part, to certain cultural expectations and academic ideals surrounding many students from other nations.

In the home context, parents of refugee and Newcomer students often bring with them stringent scholastic expectations for their children.[35] Very often, schooling in the *home* country is viewed as more rigorous and demanding than may be expected in the host country. Additionally, learning in the host country may be perceived as a direct privilege, and not to be wasted. Parents may subsequently strive for every opportunity to create successful, profitable futures for themselves and their families, and will expect their children to be a part of this charge.

Learning institutions, as well as individual teachers, can also be the source of stress for students. Teachers are accountable for student growth and success and can easily project adult performance anxieties onto students. Educators might also overwhelm learners with a heavy workload, or unnecessarily raised voices. They may expect students to attempt complicated homework (often with limited home assistance); or simply drive them crazy with teacher-personality quirks.

In addition, trauma can lead to social disorientation, which often manifests as a pronounced fear of adult authoritarian figures, including teachers.[36] Discomfort in the presence of adult authorities, consequently, can negatively impact a child's attempts to adjust and find comfort in the school setting. However, inadvertently, our tensions, demands, and simple presence can create psychological distress for our students, especially as they are expected to achieve rigorous academic outcomes in an unfamiliar language.[37]

All of this amounts to stress. We need to pause, take a breath, and be more aware of our students' strain. We can commit to growing in our practice in ways that diminish student stress and enable healthy learning. We can begin by being mindful of our adult tone and volume, and by being earnest in our trust-building efforts as we interact with each of our students, in each learning day.

Stress and Friend-Making

Stress can severely hinder trust and relationship-building capabilities, thus negatively impacting friend-making. Most Newcomer relocation efforts induce stress. Uh-oh. Here we have a challenge.

With no other complications, it may be difficult for resettled refugee children to form healthy peer relationships in the host setting.[38,39] Newcomers face challenges in communicating thoughts and feelings in the new language, and may feel that peers do not understand them. As an added complexity, children who demonstrate elements of post-traumatic stress also score lower on the *prosocial behavior* scale.[40] In other words, normative social efficacy is compromised.

When friend-making capabilities are diminished, an individual's self-esteem is also diminished. After all, we are humans; we want to be accepted, befriended, and understood. A domino effect also comes into play here. When self-esteem is in a deficit, as is a common trend among refugee students, school satisfaction and academic performance may be negatively affected. Fortunately, the opposite is also true. When our students feel strong, capable, and connected, they may also be freed to flourish in every imaginable venue.

Also, interpersonal interaction and friend-making can affect learning, specifically language acquisition. For example, a child who has difficulty recalling, pronouncing, or ordering words in the new language is likely to experience teasing or harassment. Such instances may become more frequent in the classroom, where individual responses before a student audience are commonplace. Teasing, in turn, can lead to shame and silence, and ultimately, to isolation. Such stalls create obvious fissures in an individual's friend-making capacities.[41]

Great friendships cannot be undervalued. We know this already. Now, we can add academic benefits to our list of reasons to celebrate peer friendship!

Restoration and Loss-Oriented Behaviors

Individuals exhibit two key responses to stress and transition: restoration-oriented behavior and loss-oriented behavior.[42] Both types of transitional response are exhibited in each of the resettlement domains, and can occur at varying stages throughout the resettlement process. Many factors lead to a sway toward one behavior or the other. When a particular behavior presents a majority, it may be indicative of an individual's current place (as well as future trajectory) on the integration spectrum.

Briefly, loss-oriented behaviors take effect when an individual is faced with great challenges that warrant self-preservation efforts. These reactive patterns are rooted in immediate and intense feelings of loss, disaster, and turmoil. Loss-oriented behaviors are downward spiraling.

Restoration-oriented behaviors, on the other hand, are upward spiraling. Restoration patterns typically manifest where there is calm, stability, and social support. These generally positive behaviors are associated with healthy adjustment and self-rebuilding in the host community. Restoration-oriented behaviors are a symptom of healthy integration. We can encourage restorative behaviors through modeling, direct instruction, and through consistent use of positive behavioral support systems.

REACTIVE FEAR

Fear is an inherent component of the refugee-immigrant framework. In the Newcomer setting, it is worthwhile to exercise sensitivity regarding fear-prone aspects of our individual students. I refer to the following collection of common trauma-induced reservations as The Fear List. Students who identify

---

The Fear List . . . to Fear Less
Potential Indicators for Traumatic Upset:

- Fear of Sleep
- Fear of Separation
- Fear of Trust
- Fear of Movement
- Fear of Sound
- Fear of Commotion
- Fear of Inadequate Protection
- Fear of Adults
- Fear of Close Relationships
- Fear of Long Periods of Comfort
- Fear of Solitude
- Fear of Unfamiliar Noise
- Fear of Lack
- Fear of Unknowing
- Fear of Failing
- Fear of Sharing Feelings
- Fear of Parent and Family Reaction
- Fear of Unanticipated Change
- Fear of Alarms
- Fear of Family Welfare
- Fear of being "inside the self"
- Fear of living, laughing, and living life to the fullest degree

---

Figure 3.7   Fear List

with certain elements of The Fear List are also met with opportunities to embrace, own, and eventually reconcile with life-affecting reservations. With time, these learners become *fearless*.

FRAGMENTED EDUCATION

Many of our Newcomer students will have a limited or fragmented academic history. Lapses in formal education may last for days, weeks, months, or years. These learning interruptions can occur as a singular occasion (such as an isolated breach for relocation), or at repeated intervals throughout safety-seeking resettlement efforts.[43]

A student with a history of intermittent schooling may face specific incongruities with respect to Western education. At the apex of this list is attendance. Students who come from Newcomer backgrounds are statistically more likely to be absent or tardy for school, at least in the preliminary years of adjustment.[44] We can be aware of this issue and work proactively and enthusiastically to encourage school attendance, and also set an expectation for required participation, especially within our Newcomer populations.

Another disconcerting issue for us, as teachers, is the fact that students arrive in our classrooms each year with every imaginable dearth of what we would consider "standard" academic knowledge. We can temper our anxiety by choosing to recognize the multitude of strengths that our students *do* possess, including problem-solving and critical-thinking skills that learners may already have developed expertise in. As we grow in understanding the explicit needs of our individual students, we can effectively prescribe and moderate plans to "patch the holes," meanwhile utilizing the surrounding bricks of knowledge for support and regulated structure.

HOPE AND THE RESILIENCY PHENOMENON

"Resilience is something that develops, and it only emerges as a result of adversity. Resilience . . . is the capacity for recovery."[45]

Resilient individuals have encountered high-intensity stressors that are capable of overwhelming normal function and response systems.[46, 47] Yet they have, or are in the process of, progressing through the depths of trauma and are moving forward with their life in healthy, adaptive ways. Resiliency is the marker for growth via adversity.

Resiliency is bolstered by contextual and institutional supports. Encouragingly, this ability to overcome potentially debilitating circumstances is one that can be promoted, if not explicitly taught.[48] This is great news; it indicates that *we*, as teachers, have the potentiality to guide our Newcomer students and families toward resiliency.

Resiliency has been demonstrated to respond positively to scaffolding and survival tools, as made available by adult caretakers, older siblings, or mentors.[49] Additionally, any aspect of community belongingness and engagement can promote resilience. These include intimate friend networks, access to essential services, financial security, religious networks, positive school experiences, and the presence of purposeful adult caretakers and teachers. That is, *us*.

NOTES

1. Anderson, A., Hamilton, R., Moore, D.W., Loewen, S., & Frater-Mathieson, K. (2004). Education of refugee children. Theoretical perspectives and best practice.

In Richard Hamilton & Dennis Moore (Eds.), *Educational Interventions for Refugee Children: Theoretical Perspectives and Implementing Best Practice* (pp. 1–11) UK: RoutledgeFalmer.

2. Daud, A., Britt af Klinteberg & P-A. Rydelius (2008). Resilience and Vulnerability Among Refugee Children of Traumatized Parents. *Child and Adolescent Psychiatry and Mental Health.* Vol. 2(1), No. 7.

3. Anderson, A. (2004). *Issues of Migration, in Educational Interventions for Refugee Children,* eds Richard Hamilton and Dennis Moore, (pp. 64–82). London UK: RoutledgeFalmer.

4. McBrien, J. Lynn (2003). A Second Chance for Refugee Students. *Educational Leadership* Vol. 61, No. 2, 76–9 O.

5. Ferfolja, T. & Margaret Vickers (2010). *Supporting Refugee Students in School Education in Greater Western Sydney.* School of Education, University of Western Sydney, Critical Studies in Education, Vol. 51, No. 2, 149–162.

6. Ahearn, L. M. (2011). *The Socially Charged Life of Language, in Living Language: An Introduction to Linguistic Anthropology,* Oxford, UK: Wiley-Blackwell.

7. Frater-Mathieson, K. (2004). Refugee Trauma, Loss and Grief: Implications for Intervention. In R. Hamilton & D. Moore (Eds.), *Educational Interventions for Refugee Children* (pp. 12–34). London: RoutledgeFalmer.

8. Frater-Mathieson, K. (2004). Refugee Trauma, Loss and Grief: Implications for Intervention. In R. Hamilton & D. Moore (Eds.), *Educational Interventions for Refugee Children* (pp. 12–34). London: RoutledgeFalmer.

9. Frater-Mathieson, K. (2004). Refugee Trauma, Loss and Grief: Implications for Intervention. In R. Hamilton & D. Moore (Eds.), *Educational Interventions for Refugee Children* (pp. 12–34). London: RoutledgeFalmer.

10. *Triad Mental Health. The Five Major Categories of Mental Illness.*

11. Frater-Mathieson, K. (2004). Refugee Trauma, Loss and Grief: Implications for Intervention. In R. Hamilton & D. Moore (Eds.), *Educational Interventions for Refugee Children* (pp. 12–34). London: RoutledgeFalmer.

12. Lynn, J. McBrien (2003). A Second Chance for Refugee Students. *Educational Leadership* Vol. 61, No. 2, 76–9 O.

13. Frater-Mathieson, K. (2004). Refugee Trauma, Loss and Grief: Implications for Intervention. In R. Hamilton & D. Moore (Eds.), *Educational Interventions for Refugee Children* (pp. 12–34). London: RoutledgeFalmer.

14. Lynn, J. McBrien (2003). A Second Chance for Refugee Students. *Educational Leadership* Vol. 61, No. 2, 76–9 O.

15. Ferfolja, T. & Margaret Vickers (2010). *Supporting Refugee Students in School Education in Greater Western Sydney.* School of Education, University of Western Sydney, Critical Studies in Education, Vol. 51, No. 2, 149–62.

16. Kuglar, Eileen Gale & Olga Acosta Price (2009). Go Beyond the Classroom to Help Immigrant and Refugee Students. *Phi Delta Kappan,* Vol. 91, No. 3, 48–52.

17. Frater-Mathieson, K. (2004). Refugee Trauma, Loss and Grief: Implications for Intervention. In R. Hamilton & D. Moore (Eds.), *Educational Interventions for Refugee Children* (pp. 12–34). London: RoutledgeFalmer.

18. Oberg, Dr. Kalervo (1954). *Culture Shock and the Problem of Adjustment to the New Cultural Environments.* World Wide Classroom Consortium for International Education & Multicultural studies, 2009.

19. Loewen, Shawn (2004). Second Language Concerns for Refugee Children. In R. Hamilton & D. Moore (Eds.), *Educational Interventions for Refugee Children.* London: RoutledgeFalmer.

20. Berry, J.W. & P.R. Dasen (Eds.) (1974). *Culture and Cognition: Readings in Cross-Cultural Psychology.* London: Methuen & Co.

21. Lynn, J. McBrien (2003). A Second Chance for Refugee Students. *Educational Leadership* Vol. 61, No. 2 76–9 O.

22. Lynn, J. McBrien (2003). A Second Chance for Refugee Students. *Educational Leadership* Vol. 61, No. 2 76–9 O.

23. Lynn, J. McBrien (2003). A Second Chance for Refugee Students. *Educational Leadership* Vol. 61, No. 2 76–9 O.

24. Frater-Mathieson, K. (2004). Refugee Trauma, Loss and Grief: Implications for Intervention. In R. Hamilton & D. Moore (Eds.), *Educational Interventions for Refugee Children* (pp. 12–34). London: RoutledgeFalmer.

25. Neimeyer, G.J. & F. Zaken-Greenberg (1988). The Specificity of Social-Cognitive Schemas in Interpersonal Relationships. *International Journal of Personal Construct Psychology*, 1, 139–50.

26. Frater-Mathieson, K. (2004). Refugee Trauma, Loss and Grief: Implications for Intervention. In R. Hamilton & D. Moore (Eds.), *Educational Interventions for Refugee Children* (pp. 12–34). London: RoutledgeFalmer.

27. Mehan, Hugh & Lea Hubbard, Irene Villaneuva (1994). Forming Academic Identities: Accommodation Without Assimilation Among Involuntary Minorities. *Anthropology and Education Quarterly* Vol. 25, No. 2, 91–117.

28. Anderson, A., Hamilton, R., Moore, D.W., Loewen, S., & Frater-Mathieson, K., (2004). *Education of Refugee Children: Theoretical Perspectives and Best Practice.* In *Educational Interventions for Refugee Children: Theoretical Perspectives and Implementing Best Practice*, eds R. Hamilton & D. Moore, (pp. 1–11). UK: RoutledgeFalmer.

29. Krashen, Stephen D. (1981). *Second Language Acquisition and Second Language.* University of Southern California. Pergamon Press.

30. Frater-Mathieson, K. (2004). *Refugee Trauma, Loss and Grief: Implications for Intervention.* In R. Hamilton & D. Moore (Eds.), *Educational Interventions for Refugee Children* (pp. 12–34). London: RoutledgeFalmer.

31. Ferfolja, T. & Margaret Vickers (2010). *Supporting Refugee Students in School Education in Greater Western Sydney.* School of Education, University of Western Sydney, Critical Studies in Education, Vol. 51, No. 2, 149–62.

32. Frater-Mathieson, K. (2004). Refugee Trauma, Loss and Grief: Implications for Intervention. In R. Hamilton & D. Moore (Eds.), *Educational Interventions for Refugee Children* (pp. 12–34). London: RoutledgeFalmer.

33. Frater-Mathieson, K. (2004). Refugee Trauma, Loss and Grief: Implications for Intervention. In R. Hamilton & D. Moore (Eds.), *Educational Interventions for Refugee Children* (pp. 12–34). London: RoutledgeFalmer.

34. Anderson, A. (2004). Issues of Migration. In R. Hamilton & D. Moore (Eds.), *Educational Interventions for Refugee Children* (pp. 64–82). London UK: RoutledgeFalmer.

35. Guo, Yan (2006). Why Didn't They Show Up? Rethinking ESL Parent Involvement in K-12 Education. *TESL Canada Journal* Vol. 24, No. 1.

36. Ioga, C. (1995). *The Inner Workings of the Immigrant Child.* Mahwa NJ: Lawrence Erlbaum & Associates.

37. Treuba, Enrique T. (2000). *Immigrant Voices: In Search of Educational Equity.* Maryland: Rowman & Littlefield.

38. Virtue, David C. (2009). *Serving the Needs of Immigrant and Refugee Adolescents.* Principal Publishing, Reston, Va. Vol. 89, No. 1, 64–65.

39. Loewen, Shawn (2004). Second Language Concerns for Refugee Children. In R. Hamilton & D. Moore (Eds.), *Educational Interventions for Refugee Children.* London: RoutledgeFalmer.

40. Daud, Atia, Britt af Klinteberg and Per-Anders Rydelius (2008). Resilience and Vulnerability Among Refugee Children of Traumatized Parents. *Child and Adolescent Psychiatry and Mental Health.* Vol. 2(1), No. 7.

41. Lynn, J. McBrien (2003). A Second Chance for Refugee Students. *Educational Leadership* Vol. 61, No. 2, 76–9 O.

42. Frater-Mathieson, K. (2004). Refugee Trauma, Loss and Grief: Implications for Intervention. In R. Hamilton & D. Moore (Eds.), *Educational Interventions for Refugee Children* (pp. 12–34). London: RoutledgeFalmer.

43. Ferfolja, T. & Margaret Vickers (2010). *Supporting Refugee Students in School Education in Greater Western Sydney.* School of Education, University of Western Sydney, Critical Studies in Education, Vol. 51, No. 2, 149–62.

44. DeCapua, Andrea & William Smathers, Frank Tang (2009). *Meeting the Needs of Students with Limited or Interrupted Schooling: A Guide for Educators.* University of Michigan Press.

45. Anderson, A. (2004). *Resilience.* In R. Hamilton & D. Moore (Eds.), *Educational Interventions for Refugee Children: Theoretical Perspectives and Implementing Best Practice* (pp. 53–63). London: Routledge Falmer.

46. Daud, Atia, Britt af Klinteberg & Per-Anders Rydelius (2008). Resilience and Vulnerability Among Refugee Children of Traumatized Parents. *Child and Adolescent Psychiatry and Mental Health* Vol. 2(1), No. 7.

47. Anderson, A. (2004). Resilience. In *Educational Interventions for Refugee Children: Theoretical Perspectives and Implementing Best Practice*, eds R. Hamilton & D. Moore, (pp. 53–63). London: RoutledgeFalmer.

48. Anderson, A. (2004). Resilience. In *Educational Interventions for Refugee Children: Theoretical Perspectives and Implementing Best Practice*, eds R. Hamilton & D. Moore, (pp. 53–63). London: RoutledgeFalmer.

49. Daud, Atia, Britt af Klinteberg & Per-Anders Rydelius (2008). Resilience and Vulnerability Among Refugee Children of Traumatized Parents. *Child and Adolescent Psychiatry and Mental Health* Vol. 2(1), No. 7.

Chapter 4

A Family Affair

Fostering Newcomer Family Engagement

Un asunto de familia—Spanish

OPEN DOOR POLICY

The influence that schools have on our children is all but unmatched. It is challenged only by the impact of what goes on in the home. Each school-based encounter is significant and meaningful; and each experience, in turn, is enhanced or diminished by family interaction and the nature of the home environment.

The primary role of a learning institution is to promote cognitive growth and development. However . . . have you ever tried explaining long division to a child who hasn't had breakfast? Or addressed the youngster who can't muster a grain of self-confidence in her work, because she's so embarrassed about wearing the same clothes for an entire school week? Or caught the blank stare of a fasting student who is so *over* listening?

So when and where does the learning happen here? It doesn't; at least, not wholly or effectively. There are things a child simply must have before real learning can occur, and they begin with basic needs. These include family, safety, food, clothing, and shelter. If we don't have these things for our learners, then our teaching efforts don't stand a chance.

Many of us have experienced this truth in our own classrooms. Many students present visible basic needs deficiencies in the classroom. And these are only the individuals we *know* about. How many of our learners have spent long hours in our companionship, never revealing that they are hungry or exhausted? That they work a job outside of school to help the family, or that they are recently homeless? That they couldn't sleep because their two-bedroom apartment shelters ten relatives and they couldn't find comfort on a twin mattress split four ways? Any of these are probable realities for our students—*our bright, resourceful, charismatic students.*

In many schools, on many days, even our best efforts are trumped by basic needs variables. *If* our students are properly nourished and clothed, *if* they can enjoy a sense of safety, *if* they can feel caring and belonging in the home and community, *then* they can participate in all aspects of the learning day in progressive, enjoyable ways.

PARENTS IN THE SPOTLIGHT

Parent involvement is a key indicator for academic success. Parents and caretakers are a child's very first teachers. When parents are active participants in a child's educational processes, exceptional growth can occur. In fact, caretaker partnerships with the host school and teacher are linked to learners' increased academic output, demonstrated excitement for learning, and high goal setting.[1]

Specifically in the case of Newcomer populations, "partnerships with parents can be particularly advantageous to students, especially those from economically disadvantaged families or who are ethnic minorities." Resettled refugee students are highly likely to inhabit both of these demographics, "often for the first time."[2] Healthy Newcomer-integrated schools foster positive social interchange and strong home-to-school links, even in the most dynamic conditions. Such aims, when implemented with fidelity, "are known to produce direct and positive implications for the entire initiating school organization."[3]

Not to mention that in most cases, family outreach is a legal obligation. Federal Law provides for the facilitation of parent involvement as part of 1964 legislation and the No Child Left Behind Act. Section 3302 of NCLB maintains that districts and schools that are eligible for Title III LEP funding

> shall implement an effective means of outreach to parents of limited English proficient children to inform such parents of how they can
> (A) be involved in the education of their children; and
> (B) be active participants in assisting their children
>   (i) to learn English;
>   (ii) to achieve at high levels in core academic subjects; and
>   (iii) to meet the same challenging State academic content and student academic achievement standards as all children are expected to meet.
>   [Section 3302 (e)(1)][4]

DEFINING GUARDIAN INVOLVEMENT

Parent/guardian involvement, as delineated by NCLB, refers to "the participation of parents in regular, two-way, and meaningful communication involving student academic learning and other school activities."[5] Healthy examples include asking about a child's school day, monitoring homework, creating a student workspace in the home, or reading together. Advanced involvement is evidenced through classroom volunteering and chaperoning, event participation (back-to-school nights, performances, conferences), and organized parent meetings.

Other aspects of parent-school involvement occur exclusively in the home. While these influences may not be overtly revealed to us, they can have profound impressions on classroom learning. Best practices encourage us to consider the implications of potential home learning opportunities or expertise (including the know-how of Newcomer guardians) and to expand upon and share this brand of knowledge in the school setting.

Newcomer and immigrant caretakers offer tremendous amounts of knowledge and understanding in various arenas. In most cases, this wisdom is shared with younger generations in the home. Home-based teaching may not always resemble standard instructional aims. Yet, we may be challenged to remind ourselves that lessons imparted through family can offer incredible worth and poignancy, and may be relevant to classroom learning objectives.[6]

Namely, Newcomer guardians relay critical values and skills systems. Family teachings may address morals, appropriate social exchange, cultural history, home language cultivation, and religious study. Home learning also encompasses domestic skill sets. Learning to cook, to care for younger siblings, to interact with extended family members, or to tend the home space are examples of this. Research shows an increase in Newcomer student success when parents are encouraged to demonstrate and share their unique knowledge and skills sets in the school setting, and are supported in doing so. The same practice may also support Newcomer overall parent efficacy and encourage positive feelings toward the host setting.[7]

Each of these skills has worth and significance. We empower students when we honor and elaborate upon home-based teachings within the classroom framework. This can be achieved through student share-outs, *job* assignments, tutoring activities, or leadership opportunities in an area of strength. Further, parents may be encouraged to aid overall classroom learning in an area of expertise through volunteering, mentorship, or presentation.

Whatever the degree or mechanism, caretaker involvement in students' scholastic endeavors is meaningful and impactful. The key is to acknowledge the grace and potency that is inherent to each brand of education that our children are exposed to. In our best moments, we are capable of meshing the home and school worlds. We become experts in appreciating, developing, and overlapping the two entities. In the healthiest of learning environments, guardians join their children as an integrated part of an institution's educational process. Children grow, parents are empowered, and a school is uplifted.

A PLACE TO HANG THEIR HATS: INVESTING IN PARENT COLLABORATION

We know that a whole family approach serves our students' best learning interests. We understand that community interest and involvement is a school asset with tremendous payouts. However, such presence is not instantaneous or guaranteed. Instead, it is meticulously cultivated. Who is responsible for this charge? The school and its staff. *Us.*

Strong community relations cannot occur without strong communication efforts by the school. In fact, robust school-to-home communication is an apparent quality of America's healthiest schools. Positive community outreach disseminates the breakdown of barriers between families and the school and endorses collaboration. Communication is a crux of school success, and it is one that requires support, nurturing, and creative perseverance.[8]

A school can work to foster whole family engagement in any combination of ways. The most common efforts include outreach and inclusion programs. In our classrooms, we also employ home visits, conferencing, parent/guardian correspondence, and volunteer/chaperone opportunities.[9]

The same communication tactics are applicable in Newcomer settings. However, they demand significant manipulation and elaboration in order to be successful. The truth is that home communication in multilingual, exceptionally diverse school settings doesn't always go over so smoothly. There are translations, liaisons, caseworkers, and older-child spokespersons. There are misunderstandings, misgivings, fears, and discomforts. There are frustrations, question marks, and lines of cultural jurisdiction. There is language, language, and language.

Despite obvious exchange barriers, the roots of parent-school partnership efforts are generally coherent across all socioeconomic platforms. In most cases, parents in every category *do* wish the very best for their children. Similarly, the vast majority of teachers also manifest high hopes and expectations for every single student in their care.

This is the meeting ground. Under optimal conditions, the school is synonymous with safety and collaboration. It is viewed as an action point for trustful collaboration. In the Newcomer setting, this is nonnegotiable, as many families may not be aware of or comfortable with Western academic expectations. That's a big responsibility. We must make the most of it.

SCHOOL-BASED INDUCTION PROGRAMS

A good induction is a two-way interchange between the schools and parents.[10]

Induction platforms are an inherent part of twenty-first century operation. Businesses, clubs, and other organizations incorporate induction programs as an essential preliminary function. Many schools now espouse similar initiatives. Induction programming is a best practices approach to Newcomer education, as it acts as an essential framework for positive, integrated socioacademic participation.

An exemplary Newcomer induction framework will provide for the following:

- A warm greeting and welcoming of new students and families;
- Important information about the school and school policy, using a translator and/or translated materials where possible;
- Registration assistance, with translated aid, where possible;
- School tours and classroom walk-throughs;
- Bus/pick-up instructions (including a backpack badge or other form of nonverbal identification, and a walk-through/modeling where needed);
- A peer "buddy" to help the incoming student orient to the new school environment;
- A staff or community liaison to be assigned to the new family. This person would serve as a direct contact in the school and help answer any additional questions or concerns that the parents may have;
- Guidepost resources for essential services (to be made available at the school site, whenever possible), including immunizations, dental care, reduced-cost weather-appropriate clothing, backpack and supplies assistance, among others;
- A breakdown (in the home language, when possible) of "common" academic acronyms, including IEP, ILP, PTA, DRA, ACCESS, STAR, TCAP, READ, etc.

Induction is a give and take process. The school gives, through an organized system of student admission. As personnel, we give much of ourselves through our extra efforts to be engaged and accommodating. Meanwhile, induction initiatives give back through *school* gain, and ultimately *student* gain. As an outcome of the induction process, schools acquire:

- Valuable data and background information about students and their families;
- In-person exposure to languages and preferences, both personal and cultural;
- Insight into the parents' education, students' prior education experiences, and family/social values regarding education;
- Opportunities to invite parents to become involved in adult learning, job training, and in-school volunteer programs;
- Insight into the new family's home needs, including weather-appropriate clothing, housing, and medical or food needs;
- Established sense of acceptance, belonging, safety, and partnership between the family and school.

Student and family information may be collected in written or oral questionnaire format, and it should aim to gather vital details about students' past and present school experiences, language background, home picture, and health overview. A typical questionnaire might prompt further insight into learners' (and parents') primary linguistic and cultural backgrounds; levels of English exposure and proficiency; the onset of residence in the host country; known triggers of shock or alarm; and prior experiences with host-country school systems, including parent expectation sets.[11]

Healthy Newcomer schools also facilitate an understanding of Western school and social protocol regarding education and child rearing. There are many valid means to this end, and most approaches are combined or overlapped. A short list of ideas include: parent nights, on-site adult education courses, family "adoptions" by host families or longer-resettled Newcomer families, and availability of native-language information. Access to these and similar programs can help prepare our families for unfamiliar school expectation sets in the host setting.

Induction initiatives can take some effort and perseverance to fully enact. However, the end (or rather, ongoing) product is well worth any exertion on the part of the school. In fact, the value of thorough induction cannot be understated; it is an asset to students, their families, and the entire school community.

THE WELCOMING

School staff must go out of their way to be welcoming immigrant families into the school community, for example, greeting parents in their primary language. This simple gesture can help break down the perceived walls of separation and show the parents that there is an interest in making communication easier.[12]

All schools, and Newcomer schools especially, hold an enormous responsibility to create and maintain a positive, welcoming school climate. Open inclusion efforts must permeate all aspects of the school culture, to the extent that it is radiated outward, and into the community. Sounds like some sort of metaphysical, good-in-theory sort of plan, but it is possible. In fact, it is probable under the right conditions.

Warmth and welcoming are essential cogs in the healthy, effective school machine. Smile. Say hello in the native language if possible. Be clear, organized, and gracious. Keep doors open and volumes soft. Be a safety net. Embrace fun. Smile more.

These efforts must involve *all* school personnel: administrators, teachers, librarians, custodial team, cafeteria staff, volunteers, and current students. Welcoming may be portrayed through speech, facial expressions, vocal register, and body language of school employees. It is also manifested in the cleanliness and upkeep of the school environment, including hallways, classrooms, playground and entrance. *All* of these things do matter.

A comforting welcome signals to our students and families that they are safe and valued, and that they *belong.* A sense of belonging, over time, can lead to investment and ownership. Research evidences that when families have a stake in school operations, student growth and learning success thrives.

FAMILY RESOURCE/ENGAGEMENT CENTER

A family engagement center is an asset to any school, and is of essential value to Newcomer-centered facilities. Ideally, family resources facilities are sited on the actual school campus, in a location that is easily accessible. The centers should be comfortable and welcoming, and staffed by both licensed professionals (educators, counselors, psychologists, nurses, service personnel, grant writers) and volunteers when possible.

Family engagement centers can service the school community in a variety of ways. For example, they function as adult learning and language areas, heritage and host language libraries, computer access points, job training facilities, craft centers, child care-training zones, and distribution centers (for school supplies, clothing and other essential items, particularly for students shifting into a colder environment, or parents who will be interviewing for new jobs). Most schools and districts with high ELL populations have or plan to have operative resource centers that are free and accessible to the parents and families of ELL students.

THE PAPERWORK PREDICAMENT

Understandably, many Newcomer families will experience distress or frustration with regard to navigating copious amounts of school-originated paperwork. The fate of most homebound correspondence: "My mom or dad don't know how to read English, so they just threw it away. Nobody at my home understands what it says." That doesn't help much.

Most Newcomer students acknowledge that parents are more inclined to read materials that are translated into the home language. Still, even translations may be unreliable in terms of accuracy and clarity, especially in circumstances where educational acronyms and other jargon are used (hello, PARCC, SAT, ACCESS, CELA). New layers of complexity are added when administrative documents are sent home requiring signatures, appointment scheduling, and provision of important family data.

Nonetheless, translation efforts can jump certain fences and produce positive returns. If the entire document cannot be translated, it is ideal to have a standard top-form in multiple languages signaling the necessity of having the document interpreted by another person. Most Newcomer schools and multi-language districts have already adopted this (or a similar) form of paperwork policy. Wherever possible, important messages should be communicated in person, via outreach protocol. Finally, schools and teachers should avoid sending home any unnecessary literature.

ELA and LEP (limited English proficient) families require and deserve certain accommodations for homebound correspondence, and we should do our best to be considerate of these realities. As schools and school districts prepare such documents, it is important to consider language and culture barriers which may or may not exist in a child's home. If we are able to reduce or eliminate certain family stressors that are related to overwhelming school memos, then we are able to reserve caretaker energies for other, more meaningful engagements.

HOME VISITS

Home visits are a very tangible means of connecting with families. Sure, home visits can feel awkward, uncomfortable, and time-consuming. Yet, they can also be immensely rewarding and vitally revealing. Ultimately, home visits can promote mutual understanding and connectivity between the family and the classroom environments.

Home visits are the first line of intermediation between the home and the school, and are very often teacher-initiated. This *front-line* approach has especial significance in working with Newcomer refugee and immigrant families. One reason for this is that a high number of Newcomer families are without personal transportation required to reach the school conveniently or safely, thus, severely curbing parent-teacher contact. Such limitations can be alleviated via home visits.

A teacher's first attempts to visit students' homes—especially Newcomer homes, which are likely in highly impoverished project areas—can feel overwhelming. These efforts are rife with challenges, as they force us to negotiate the unfamiliar: directions, languages, cultural miscues, and personal discomfort. With time, however, the visitation process becomes more natural, and it often culminates in profound benefits for both the visitor and hosts.

We can make it a point to visit at least one or two student homes per academic year (of course, it is always wise to go accompanied). Chances are, those *one or two* will turn into five or six . . . or ten or twelve. This is a ball that can get rolling quickly.

When a guest (such as a teacher) is visiting, most Newcomer families give immensely through hosting. While the likelihood is that our families possess very little in their initial years, it will be their cultural custom to gift food, drink, or other items as tokens of appreciation and respect. It is unlikely that we will leave a student's home disappointed or regretful. Rather, with each instance, we might feel inspired and also slightly more grounded and better equipped to teach from a place of personal experience, compassion, and cultural cognizance.

Each home visit presents a chance to digest a little bit more about what the learners' past and present home lives entail. Home visitations expose opportunities to fine-tune instruction and more precisely meet individual student needs, which may be very specific to home, family, and cultural background. Moreover, teacher presence in the home nurtures and solidifies student-to-teacher relationships and provides a tangible, coherent link to the school entity.

HOME-TO-SCHOOL JOURNALS

Home-to-school journals are beneficial instruments for teachers, students, and caretakers. For educators, student journaling can provide valuable insights into the student's home life and culture, meanwhile allowing for formative assessment of learners' vocabulary and writing progress. For students, home-to-school journals allow for less formal practice with language expression, promote student creativity, and can serve as a therapeutic outlet.

Caretakers can benefit when home-to-school journals are also designed to incorporate parent access and feedback. This form of interactive journaling can provide adults in the home the ability to reinforce important information, inform parents of behavioral concerns, and provide them with a better idea of what their children are working to accomplish at school.

Of course, journaling in the Newcomer setting requires ELL modifications and scaffolding. Start slowly. Even the most simplified forms of written expression, including picture drawing and labeling, successfully serve the intended purpose.

MAKING ROOM FOR THE HOME CULTURE IN THE CLASSROOM

An ELL's family and cultural community life provide them with a rich history and a connection with people who hold many shared fundamental values and experiences. The ESL child's school world often revolves around concepts and ideas that are greatly disconnected from their home life and may even be contradictory in values and experiences.[13]

The idea of kinship is important to most cultures in the world, and is often paramount among refugee demographics. Kinship refers to socio-familial interchange that extends beyond the nuclear organism. In this context, relationship roles are implicitly established, with generally unwavering consistency, according to shared lineage, proximity, or ingrained cultural values. Kinship, then, operates as the basis for extended family and community cohesiveness.

Refugees and immigrants have higher resettlement success rates when they are part of a kinship network in the host settings. Kinship in the host setting endorses stability, structure, and a sense of safety; and it serves to perpetuate heritage culture and value systems. Mutually shared experiences, such as cooking traditional foods together, attending religious services, honoring special holidays, and celebrating shared interests strengthen and reveal inherent social structures that are essential for healthy transition.[14]

Kinship factors can also positively influence our students' social and scholastic success. Newcomer students who *do* maintain important connections to their host culture demonstrate a strengthened propensity for healthy acculturation and scholastic aptitude in the new country. We can help students to merge the home and host cultures, even as part of the routine school day. We do this by empowering the heritage culture and home values, while explicitly teaching key values, social norms, and respect for the host country. In the most vibrant and capable school settings, heritage pride can exist in a peaceful, multifaceted, all-embracing capacity.

THE NATIVE-LANGUAGE PIECE

Continued native-language learning in the home is likely to *positively* influence host-country academic success. In fact, heritage culture sacrifice, including linguistic detachment, may hinder a person's healthy self-view, and consequently impact one's ability to interact and integrate in constructive, holistic ways. Self-esteem and self-confidence are determining factors in a young person's ability to experience social and academic achievement. Intact cultural identity and related self-integrity can actually act as a buffer against trauma, subsequently increasing the likelihood of healthy assimilation into the host culture.[15]

We can be active champions for home culture and language preservation, especially with regard to refugees and immigrants. In doing so, we should be careful not to entirely restrict first language practice, even as it occurs simultaneously with host language education. We can give parents verbal approval to maintain heritage cultures and languages in the home. Expert Lucy Tse writes, "It seems that language minority families need to have permission to know that using their first language is a positive at so many levels."[16] How true!

We can make a point to become invested in our students' diversity by honoring and supporting heritage cultures and languages in the classroom. Through this, we become responsible for paving healthy avenues toward host-setting inclusion. When we are able to celebrate the whole child, we are also architects of esteem and confidence. In the process, we can make room for the 8,693 teachable moments that follow suit!

ALLEVIATING PARENT-TEACHER DISCONNECTS

One of the major challenges that Newcomer schools face is overcoming real (and perceived) disconnects between the caretakers and the school staff. Parents—and Newcomer parents, specifically—might be reluctant to approach school personnel for any number of reasons. It should be our aim to work toward eliminating these obstructions and problem solving for creative accommodation strategies for our Newcomer families.

Of course, a paucity of English communication abilities is a key challenge. Language barriers can produce other side effects, which may include diminished self-confidence in approaching school staff, insensitivity on the part of school staff, or prior negative experiences in the school setting. Also, many parents encounter work, transportation or childcare issues that prevent them from having an active school presence.

There may also be some cultural misalignment regarding home and host educational values and expectation systems. Parents and guardians of New-comer students may experience confusion, disenchantment, or disappoint-ment with Western approaches. Adult Newcomers may compare a child's education in the new country with their own academic experiences in the home country.

Many resettled parents will recall longer school days in the native country. They may also be familiar with fewer recesses and vacations, intensive home-work sessions, oral rote drills, and stiff discipline in the school place (includ-ing physical and verbal punishments). As a result, parents may feel that host education is not as strict, strenuous, or cognitively demanding as they might have hoped or anticipated.[17]

It is important to keep in mind that many of our Newcomer students did, in fact, have access to early education or homeschool education in the first (or second or third) country. In fact, our students' academic workload may have been *more* intense and demanding in their heritage scenarios. With this in mind, Newcomer guardians frequently request *additional* homework for their child. They may also request that we exercise more firmness in disciplining their child.

We can counter these misunderstandings through patient explanation, through a translator, where appropriate. Parents may feel more at ease when the direction and reasoning for a given curricula is made explicitly clear to them, and also when we open the doors for parents to be partners in host-setting instructional aims. Also, we can be diligent in maintaining a high degree of rigor in every aspect of the school day.

TEACHER AS EXPERT

Another key point of contention is rooted in *the teacher as an expert* percep-tion. In most non-Western cultures, educators are highly regarded as essential pillars of the community.[18] The teacher, in these societies, is considered a sole authority in terms of all learners' academic welfare. Thus, education is considered the singular responsibility of the teacher. As a matter of trust and respect, parents are socially deterred from interfering with this process. New-comer parents who are accustomed to this scenario will be highly unlikely to question the role or actions of a teacher, as such infringements would be considered offensive and disrespectful.[19, 20]

Complications occur when this behavior, as viewed in the West, may resemble a "lack" of parental involvement or disinterest in a child's learning.

We may become frustrated or affronted. However, the families themselves probably believe *they are doing the right thing.* Indeed, the concept of parent involvement in education is almost exclusively a North American one.

Finally, some parents will feel distress regarding their child's *Newcomer* placement. They may be very anxious to see their child mainstreamed, reasoning that English-focused classrooms might deprive their child from learning essential core curriculum. There may also exist a paranoia that language-sheltered education will deter or postpone grade-appropriate instruction.[21]

In effort to counter this, and other misconceptions, we must share in the responsibility of opening healthy lines of communication between the home and the school. In doing so, we make room for understanding, cooperation, and collaboration. When we, as host educators, are better informed, we're less likely to react out of confusion or insult. Instead, we might be more inclined to respond with compassion, understanding, and careful planning.

Our host normative mentality, to Newcomers, equates to a foreign set of regulations and expectations that must be deliberately introduced and explicitly taught as part of standard curricula. Parent involvement is likely to be among these key foreign nuances, and it is our obligation to reframe school participation expectations, so as to benefit student learning and family integration. Even when such involvement is against the natural grain of a heritage culture, parent involvement can provide innumerable lasting benefits for the school and its students. Simply, whole family engagement influences students' academic success in profound ways.

It truly *does* take a village, and our classrooms are city centers.

NOTES

1. Epstein, J.L. (1994). *Perspectives and Previews on Research and Policy for Schools, Family and Community Partnerships.* Penn. State University.

2. D. Moore (Eds.), *Educational Interventions for Refugee Children* (pp. 35–52). London: RoutledgeFalmer.

3. Hamilton, R. & D. Moore (2004). Schools, Teachers and Education of Refugee Children, In *Educational Interventions for Refugee Children: Theoretical Perspectives and Implementing Best Practice,* eds R. Hamilton & D. Moore, London: Routledge Falmer.

4. No Child Left Behind Act 3302, Section E (2015). U.S. Department of Education. Located at www2.ed.gov/policy/elsec/leg/esea02/pg50.html. Retrieved Feb 2015.

5. No Child Left Behind Act. U.S. Department of Education. Located at www2.ed.gov/policy/elsec/leg/esea02/pg50.html. Retrieved Feb 2015.

6. Hamilton, R. & D. Moore (2004). Schools, Teachers and Education of Refugee Children. In *Educational Interventions for Refugee Children: Theoretical*

Perspectives and Implementing Best Practice, eds R. Hamilton & D. Moore, London: Routledge Falmer.

7. Bridging Refugee Youth & Childrens Services (BRYCS) (2007). *Involving Refugee Parents in Their Children's Education.* Located at brycs.org. Retrieved May 2014.

8. Chadha, N.K. (PhD) (2015). *Intergenerational Relationships: An Indian Perspective.* Department of Psychology, University of Delhi. Located at un.org. Retrieved Aug 2015.

9. Kuglar, E. Gale & Olga Acosta Price (2009). Go Beyond the Classroom to Help Immigrant and Refugee Students. *Phi Delta Kappan*, Vol. 91, No. 3, 48–45.

10. Ferfolja, T. & M. Vickers (2010). *Supporting Refugee Students in School Education in Greater Western Sydney.* School of Education, University of Western Sydney, Critical Studies in Education, Vol. 51, No. 2, 149–62.

11. Detzner, D. (2010). *Background on South East Asian Parenting.* College of Human Ecology, University of Minnesota Press.

12. Ferfolja, T. & M. Vickers (2010). *Supporting Refugee Students in School Education in Greater Western Sydney.* School of Education, University of Western Sydney, Critical Studies in Education, Vol. 51, No. 2, 149–62.

13. Ferfolja, T. & Margaret Vickers (2010). *Supporting Refugee Students in School Education in Greater Western Sydney.* School of Education, University of Western Sydney, Critical Studies in Education, Vol. 51, No. 2, 149–62.

14. Kuglar, E. Gale & Olga Acosta Price (2009). Go Beyond the Classroom to Help Immigrant and Refugee Students. *Phi Delta Kappan*, Vol. 91, No. 3, 48–52.

15. Loewen, S. (2004). Second Language Concerns for Refugee Children. In *Educational Interventions for Refugee Children,* eds R. Hamilton & D. Moore, (pp. 35–52). London: RoutledgeFalmer.

16. Tse, L. (2001). *Why Don't They Learn English? Separating Fact from Fallacy in the U.S. Language Debate.* New York Teachers College Press.

17. Loewen, S. (2004). Second Language Concerns for Refugee Children. In *Educational Interventions For Refugee Children,* eds R. Hamilton & D. Moore, (pp. 35–52). London: RoutledgeFalmer.

18. Ng, E. *Supporting Families and Developing Parent Leaders Among The Immigrant Chinese Community in Boston.* In VUE Journal, Annenberg Institute for School Reform, pp. 38–46. Located at annenberginstitute.org. Retrieved Aug 2015.

19. Virginia Department of Education, Division of Instruction (2006). *English: Strategies for Teaching Limited English Proficient (LEP) Students.* Located at doe.virginia.gov. Retrieved May 2012.

20. Hamilton, R. & D. Moore (2004). Schools, Teachers and Education of Refugee Children. In *Educational Interventions for Refugee Children: Theoretical Perspectives and Implementing Best Practice*, eds R. Hamilton & D. Moore, London: Routledge Falmer.

21. Moore, D., Conceptual Policy Issues. In *Educational Interventions for Refugee Children: Theoretical Perspectives and Implementing Best Practice*, eds Richard Hamilton & Dennis Moore, London: RoutledgeFalmer.

Chapter 5

Cultural (Mis)Understandings

ការយល់ច្រឡំវប្បធម៌ -Khmer

EXAMINING CUSTOM & CULTURAL NUANCES

Authentic cultural tolerance and understanding is a fundamental basis for success in the Newcomer classroom. A willingness to maintain awareness and open-mindedness in culturally divergent settings can promote positive exchange and individual growth. When we are able to engage with our students from bases of respect, tolerance, and attempted understanding, we also foster reciprocation of these same traits back onto ourselves, and also toward classroom peers. If, on the other hand, we develop habits of projecting fear, misinterpretation, and bias onto our pupils, then we have also contaminated the entire sanctity of the learning environment.[1,2]

We know that the ways in which we view and interact with our students can tremendously influence students' classroom and learning success.[3] With regard to tolerance and cultural respect, every lesson begins with ourselves. Our behaviors will be modeled long before, and long after, our words have an opportunity to make an impression.

Our efforts to teach cultural sensitivity are enabled when we have also identified and made peace with our own intolerances. In this way, we can actively and honestly promote organic strands of intercultural and interhuman respect. Authentic tolerance is indeed a key launch point in advocating for healthy learning environments.

Realistically, however, and despite our best efforts, it can still be difficult, confusing, or unsettling to come into contact with cultural tendencies that are unfamiliar to us. In the Newcomer setting, there are many, many opportunities for this precise challenge to occur.

Indeed, our Newcomer students may prove among the richest, most experienced cultural guides that we will know.

One specific conundrum is the eye contact issue. In the Newcomer setting, it is very common to encounter students who stoutly refuse to look an adult in the eye when they are being spoken to. This behavior may be especially evident if a child is being pointed out or reprimanded. In the West, direct eye contact with an adult or elder is typically equated with respect and obedience. Therefore, a dismissive look signals defiance and disinterest. This is *our* truth.

However, direct eye contact between a child and an adult is considered atypical behavior in many of the world's cultures. Throughout East and North Africa, for example, direct eye contact between a child and elder is considered a sign of intense disrespect on the part of the youth. Resettled persons from these regions will very likely instruct their own children to look down when speaking to anyone older or of greater perceived importance, as this is what is considered the honorable thing to do.

Aha! Our eye contact-avoiding students, whom we may have perceived as acting disrespectfully, have been demonstrating utmost respect all along. These individuals exhibit respect via *their* truths, and according to personal experiences and relative social norms. There you have it. The teacher is just not always right.

Other cultural nuances are also evidenced in the classroom. For instance, many East Asian and Arab students are noticeably consumed with the notion of *losing face*. That is, they strive to avoid even the slightest run-in with public humiliation, especially that which would bring shame to the greater family unit.

This phenomenon surrounding fear of failure typically prevents risk taking, volunteering, and sometimes even *trying* in the classroom. Educators who come from a background of outspoken Western idealism may experience frustration at recurrent student episodes of superfluous caution. We might expect or wish that our learners would *simply* take a chance; to speak out, speak up, and care just a little less about peer judgment and evaluation.

From a culturally mindful perspective, meanwhile, we see that for most Newcomers, family and community comprise the very heart of a meaningful life. To embarrass or shame the family name could result in shunning either of the individual by the family, or the family by the community. Both fates equate to social death. Excellence and recognition, on the other hand, can bring respect and glory to an entire family and community.

In terms of social cohesiveness and support in the post-resettlement context, there are certain advantages to the *saving face* mentality. This inherent code of honor serves as a binding agent for resettled ethnic populations.

It may serve as a cohesive strand between culturally diverse ethnic populations, as well.

In the classroom, students who had been taught to adhere to *saving face* principals are very frequently self-driven learners who diligently applied themselves to their studies in an extended effort to bring happiness and honor to the home. They are likely to hesitate in answering questions, unless they can be absolutely certain that they have the correct response, and they may strive to please the teacher in every possible way. We can guide these students toward classroom chance taking by providing a nurturing classroom environment and celebrating mistakes as opportunities for continued growth.

We will face many challenges in recognizing, interpreting, and accepting our students' many cultural qualities. No one approach to living or learning necessarily trumps another. Each is simply *different.*

In the end, it is not a student's sole responsibility to change to suit the teacher's needs. Unquestionably, our Newcomers will be required to learn and adopt many westernized customs in order to successfully assimilate into our culture. As educators, we can also allow ourselves some room for adjustment. These small personal transformations are reflected in the positive and tolerant ways that we choose to interact with students and plan for their optimal learning in each school day.

CULTURE AND CLASSROOM IMPLICATIONS

A number of culturally divergent behaviors play out in the Newcomer ELA-E classroom. For example, acceptable distances of physical proximity, vocal volume norms, pleasantry tactics and privacy stipulations can dramatically swing from one cultural demographic to another. Many other examples stand out. Most will be relevant to the classroom setting. It is impossible to notice and make sense of all of our students' culturally divergent tendencies. We can begin by developing an awareness of certain key factions, as shown in Figure 5.2.

It is worthwhile to explore some of these tendencies in greater depth. When we train ourselves to notice cultural nuances, we can also respond to them appropriately. In this way, we can ensure that loss of learning time is limited and student growth is enhanced.

LEFT HAND AS ABOMINATION

In many non-westernized cultures, the use of the left hand is considered *unclean* and is strictly avoided in any social setting. Eating, passing objects, hand holding, patting, or greeting with the left hand may be considered taboo.

observable

- body movements
- facial expressions
- volume and tone
- eye contact

- gestures
- housing
- dress
- material interest

interpersonal

- concept of self
- concept of space
- tone and volume
- friendship
- courtship

- social etiquette
- view of authority figures
- problem-solving sets
- normative social cues
- social/ media preferences

values & ideals

- male/female roles
- concept of time
- leadership
- education
- fairness
- importance of work

- child-rearing
- concept of beauty
- past/future relationships
- acts of perceived abomination
- hesitancy & uniformity

custom

- food and eating behaviors
- holidays
- theory of dependents
- language
- adolescent markers
- shared world view

- interaction with elders
- relation to nature
- religious beliefs and rituals
- ambiguity

art

- song & dance
- drama
- textiles
- crafts & weaving
- written word & poetry

Figure 5.2   Culturally Divergent Tendencies

It is wise to be cognizant of this when presenting children or parents with pencils, paper, or treats with the left hand; the act may be received as inauspicious or as an outright abomination. Also, children who may be naturally left-handed go to great lengths to avoid using this hand for writing or other activities in the classroom, and quality of work may be impacted as a result.

ASKING FOR AID

Asking for help is not encouraged in most East Asian school settings. This may occur for several reasons. The first has to do with the concept of *saving face*, in which an individual may feel personal shame or greater family shame for not understanding. Second, asking questions often denotes individualism, which is rarely a prized value in Eastern cultures. Finally, in many countries, the teacher is considered the expert and authority in all matters relating to education, and therefore, it may be perceived as disrespectful to ask a teacher for clarification on a subject. As a potential result of heritage customs, the concept of asking for aid may require explicit modeling in the host setting.

WANDER-AND-EXPLORE TENDENCIES

Many cultures place great emphasis on the need for children to learn through exploration and experience. Even the very young are encouraged to experiment, play, and seek answers in a very tangible sense, often apart from direct adult supervision. In some communities, practical education is regarded with as much or more reverence than structured book learning. The tools, ingenuity, and skill sets that children gather during this adventurous time often enable future work and survival success, thus serving as an asset to the community as a whole.[4]

This is in direct conflict with traditional Western *Sit-Up-Straight-And-Tall* methodology. As a result, students who are more accustomed to wander-and-explore learning may have a very challenging time adjusting to certain classroom norms in the host setting. We're talking about that child who seems entirely *allergic* to a desk chair. The one who stands as he or she writes, whose shoes have a habit of magically evading his or her actual feet, and whose desk is a nesting place for pen caps, twigs, puffballs, marbles, and origami triangles—that just might be your *Wander-And-Explore* student.

And it's ok. These students are still learning, after all! Typically, these harmless classroom behaviors will dissipate with time. Again, they are not wrong; they are just different than what we have been trained to be used to. Best practices call for us to provide explicit learning opportunities for wander-and-explore learners that accentuate their problem-solving strengths, such as manipulative learning techniques. Meanwhile, we can promote positive behaviors that will lend to their future success in westernized schooling environments.

PERSONAL SPACE AND PRIVACY CONSIDERATIONS

In many countries and cultures, personal space is not valued as a commodity. In these settings, spatial boundaries may be nonexistent. It will be very natural for students from these regions to position themselves extremely close to other individuals throughout the school day. Custom may encourage students to push right up to another student while standing in line, or think little of physical contact such as touching elbows or knees at a desk. Talking may occur at close range.

These behaviors are a routine part of life in many African and Middle Eastern countries. They are, in their essence, innocent reflections of human nature, in contexts where many people share a limited space. However, privacy considerations can become problematic in the classroom when someone with contrasting personal space values encounters them. Spatial consideration may require explicit teaching and modeling within the classroom.

ADHERENCE TO TIME

Time is not regarded with the same level of importance in all parts of the world. In the westernized sense, timeliness is considered a virtue, and adherence to time is the common norm. In many cultures, however, timeliness may be outvalued by social interaction and other obligations.

In most African countries and many regions of East Asia and Central and South America, for example, it is considered extremely rude to cut greetings or exchanges short in an effort to make an appointment deadline, or for any other reason. Thus, meetings and other professional or social engagements can run far behind schedule. Lateness, in most cases, is not considered rude or irresponsible. Loose adherence to time is merely a reflection of cultural values. Therefore, punctual behavior may need to be overtly encouraged in the Western setting.

VOLUME AND TONE

Normative values for conversational volume can vary drastically between cultures. Vocal registers that may be customary to many Middle Eastern or African cultures may feel harsh or alarming, at least according to Western expectations. In many regions, verbal exchange is an animated and lively process, and volume considerations may not be as esteemed as they are in the host setting. Meanwhile, Latin American or East Asian volume norms may be seem diminutive in contrast to host values, as soft speech and inwardness are considered virtuous character traits. In the classroom context, we need to work with our learners in establishing volume norms that are conducive to social and learning success.

UNIFORMITY

Individualism is a trend that is largely exclusive to Western cultures. Most other countries celebrate collectivism, which encourages viewing the self as inherently and wholly linked to surrounding bands of community, beginning with the family. This whole-group perspective serves to motivate decision making that will positively influence not only the self, but also the entire social dynamic.

Learners who are accustomed to uniformity value systems may find little appeal in standing out in the classroom setting. They may have limited desire to be *the best*, or to ask for help or clarification. Blending into the overall group dynamic is seen as a definitive honor and benefit to the family and cultural group.

We can guide our students and families to enjoy some of the benefits that individualism can provide in the host environment. Ultimately, we hope for a balance. Students will need to exercise some elements of independence in order to fully thrive in the twenty-first-century learning environment; and they may also be compelled to retain certain heritage values. We can do our best as educators by honoring both avenues, as well as all the gray areas in between!

"I AM FROM . . ."

In my first year of teaching in the Newcomer sector, I remember feeling flabbergasted by one very real truth: our little four-walled classroom housed the world inside its perimeter. Out of the twenty-five students that first year, fourteen countries were represented in our classroom, with nineteen first languages among them. I still cherish this memory, and perhaps more so now that I've also acquired some understanding of the unique countries, customs, and languages that we have in our care.

I arrived as head of the classroom that year, the first year that our refugee-magnate school was set in motion, highly unprepared. I was fresh, sure, and knowledgeable in the field of education, too. I was also remarkably naïve. Armed with personal monologues of out-of-country experiences, I thought I was worldly, exposed, and ready. Then, I *got schooled* by a class of eight-year-olds.

When, for example, students stated, "I am from Burma," I assumed, well, Burma. As in, one Burma, the one I located on Google Maps (just to refresh my memory . . . of course). As in, one culture, one language, one struggle, one united journey to our classroom.

That episode of simplistic thinking was short-lived. Within days, I figured out that several of my Burmese students couldn't actually communicate orally with each other. Moreover, this group of students did not always appear outwardly friendly toward one another, despite their apparent cultural similarities. In fact, I was noticing intense tensions and aggressions between like-cultured groups, even while cross-cultural communications remained friendly and outgoing.

At one point early in the year, Snay Doh came to see me in private. He asked to move his seat away from his Thai peer, Thaw Eh Htoo. He wished to sit at a separate desk, between Valentin from Burundi, and Khaled from Yemen. "I don't mind thinking about this, Snay Doh," I replied, "but I hope that you can explain to me why this is a good idea. Moving your seat isn't going to make a bigger problem go away. What is it that seems to be keeping you and Thaw from getting along?"

Snay Doh, with his limited English vocabulary, broke down the entire dilemma, with Crayola illustrations and all. In the end, I learned that Snay Doh's parents were Burma-Burmese, and that he was born in the refugee camps in Thailand. Thaw Eh Htoo was also born in a Thai refugee camp. However, his parents were Karen Burmese. Not only were these two families from geographically, linguistically, and culturally separate parts of Burma; they were also at war with one another.

With a little more research, I came to realize that four rivers physically separate the small nation of Burma into five distinct geographical regions. Within these regions, a multitude of individual tribes maintain separate and exclusive lifestyles and cultures. Seven of these tribes demand high social and political prominence. These clans have an epic history of interaction, often involving warfare on every level and for every reason: territory, religion, water, trade, and government.

Members from five of these tribes held places on that first year roster. So, no; that original seating arrangement with four of those Burmese students, of four separate religions, customs and dialects at the same table didn't work out so well. (Enter school-wide positive behavior system roll-out.)

Similar dichotomies are repeated each year in our little school room, and are reflected in the lives of our students from all over the world: Congo, Iran,

Somalia, and Libya, and many others. The truth is that people who originate from one country are not necessarily homogeneous, or for that matter, oozing with camaraderie with one another. Fundamental views and values may vary dramatically, even to the point of enmity. For me, this lesson was critical. Indeed, we are never done learning.

AS THE CROW FLIES

Interestingly, our students' documented countries of origination are rarely aligned with actual ancestral roots. This occurs primarily because many of our students are transported to (or even born in refugee camps) proximal to the heritage region.[5]

For example, most *Nepali* refugees are Bhutanese. Many *Thai* students are Burmese. Our *Kenyan* students might be exclusively Congolese, Somalian, Rwandan, or Ethiopian. A *Syrian* student's first home may have been Iraq, Afghanistan, Jordan, or Lebanon.

Sometimes a spade is a spade; Congo really does mean Congo, and there is no need to complicate things further. But often, it doesn't hurt to engage in a little sleuthing. The results can be astonishing. Frequently, Newcomers will have lived in a multitude of nations, even leading up to the country of origin that appears on resettlement documentation. This information can be helpful, in that it allows for additional insights into students' probable cultural and learning backgrounds. It might also sway us away from topical assumptions and approaches to our craft. Cultural geography 101, via the wide-eyed testimonies of our learners.

The list below indicates possible refugee origination locales. The perimeter countries represent heavily documented home nations. The adjacent regions are plausible induction zones. Often, grouped nations may be interchanged as first, second, or third origination countries. Of course, this resource equates to a rough-sketch approximation guide. The only true authorities on our students' pre-resettlement paths are our students and families themselves.

POTENTIAL REFUGEE ORIGINATION LOCALES

Nepal: Bhutan, Tibet

India: Iran, Nepal, Bhutan, Tibet, Bangladesh, Sri Lanka, Afghanistan, and China

Kenya: Congo, Uganda, Rwanda, Burundi, Somalia, Sudan, and Ethiopia

Ghana: Ivory Coast, Burkina Faso, Liberia, Togo, Benin, Mali, Nigeria, and Senegal

Egypt: Eritrea, Ethiopia, Sudan, South Sudan, Somalia, Libya, Syria, Djibouti, Uganda, Rwanda, Burundi, Yemen, Congo, and Lebanon

Libya: Tunisia, Lebanon, Syria, Eritrea, Sudan, Senegal, Egypt, Somalia, Uganda, Rwanda, Burundi, Congo, Yemen, Djibouti, and Algeria

Thailand, Malaysia: Myanmar Burma, Karen Burma, Chin Burma, Cambodia, Laos, Vietnam, and China

Bangladesh: Rohingya Burma, Urdu Pakistan, Iran, Philippines, and Vietnam

Jordan: Iraq, Syria, Lebanon, Palestine, Ethiopia, Tunisia, Armenia, Bosnia, Serbia, and Afghanistan

Turkey: Russia, Iraq, Iran, Syria, Lebanon, Uzbekistan, Tajikistan, Kazakhstan, Pakistan, Kyrgyzstan

Brazil: Venezuela, Honduras, Paraguay, Ecuador, Columbia, and Costa Rica

Mexico: Costa Rica, Guatemala, Haiti, Jamaica, Columbia, Venezuela, Brazil, Argentina, Honduras, and Chili.

CULTURAL INTRICACIES (SORT OF) EXPLAINED

Pinpointing our students' point(s) of origination is merely a launch pad for understanding. Next, if we are so inclined, there are infinite corridors of cultural nuances to explore. While in-depth detective work is impractical, even a slight knowledge or shown interest can work wonders in sparkling lasting student-teacher relationships.

Many of our learners are active participants in multiple cultures. This is common in the macro-micro-culture context. In this case, a local tribe maintains a very distinct set of traditional customs, which are vastly different from the overriding national exchange customs.

This occurs frequently in Africa and the Far East. For example, the *Myanmar Chin* tribe maintains a set of language, dress, agricultural, ceremonial, and culinary codes that are invariably separate from overriding Burmese culture. Yet, members of the Chin tribe must possess a knowledge of, and fluidity within, the Burmese mainstream in order to achieve social mobility.

In the same way, resettled learners who identify with a shared origination country may be intrinsically dissimilar with regard to custom, etiquette, language, and background skill sets. The Democratic Republic of Congo, for example, is comprised of over 200 exceptionally distinct tribes and over 700 languages and dialects. Most inhabitants are fluent in French, and can converse with neighboring tribes in an additional four to six tongues. Individual tribes offer additional layers of history and social functionality. Therefore, it is wrong to assume that two students who are from the same country will naturally understand or relate to one another.

CULTURAL NUANCE FRAMEWORK

The following guide is designed to facilitate teacher-student and teacher-parent interaction. It can serve as a wide-ranging resource for identifying and assessing culturally specific student behaviors. It is also a reliable tool for navigating parent-teacher conferences and other family-centered school events.

As a reminder, there is no blanketed application for this or any other instrument of global understanding. Every student's story is different, and every Newcomer's cultural cloth is inimitable. Further, family and individual personality can override cultural influence.

Similarly, it would be irresponsible to suggest that countries that are grouped together on this map are also identical in their customs or cultural composite. This is not the aim, and could not be further from the truth. Individual countries, and specific regions within those countries, are capable of vast discrepancies from one another.

Nonetheless, many combined countries and cultures within a shared geographic region will enjoy certain overarching societal values and norms. This is precisely what is offered here: a broad reflection of probable tendencies for a given population, and a snapshot of humanity in the different corners of our globe. These are tools, and they construct a useful start!

GENERALIZED CULTURAL NUANCES, BY REGION

Syria, Kuwait, Iraq, Libya, Jordan:

- Extended family is the basis of self and the external social structure.
- A handshake or exchanged kisses on the cheek are standard greetings. It may be unacceptable for a man to instigate a physical greeting with a woman; a slight bow with a hand on the chest is the norm. Direct eye contact is anticipated.
- Conversation may become loud and animated—this is not usually a sign of distress. Direct expressive confrontation is usually avoided.
- Personal space is honored; arm's length distancing is the norm. Public displays of affection are discouraged. Same-sex persons commonly join arms or hands as a sign of friendship and comradery.
- Timeliness is not always honored, or necessarily considered a virtue.
- Clicking of the tongue, raised eyebrows, or a back tilt of the head indicate "no."

- Pride and honor are very important; great efforts are taken to avoid public embarrassment or humiliation of the self or family name. Showing of emotions is viewed negatively, as a means of preserving dignity.
- Soles of the feet should not be shown or pointed at any person, as they are the lowest part of the body. Pointing should be done with the whole hand, not an isolated finger.
- In Islamic contexts, Friday is considered a holy day, and Thursday is its precursor. Thus, these two days are considered the weekend.
- Practicing Muslims are required to fast from dawn to dusk each day during the month of Ramadan. While younger children are usually exempt from this, fasting older students may have a difficult time with concentration and alertness.
- Naming is systematic. The first name is a personal one; the second is the name of the father; the third and fourth relate the name of the grandfather and the specific tribe. Names are connected with "Al" or "El," meaning "of" (son of, grandson of). Women often do not take the husband's name after marriage.
- Exceptional hospitality is expected. Gifts are usually not opened at the time they are received.
- Eating should occur with only the right hand. Genders may dine in separate rooms.
- Keeping of one's word is of extremely high importance.
- The right hand to the chest indicates, "Thanks, but no thanks."
- Shoes may need to be removed when entering a home.

Burma, Cambodia, Thailand

- Family forms the cornerstone of life; respect for parents and elders is expected. Superior/inferior roles are enforced, including the teacher-student hierarchy.
- The standard greeting is a handshake or a slight bow or handshake with hands in prayer fashion. The higher the hands and lower the bow, the deeper the gesture of respect. Punctuality is considered a positive personality trait.
- Exchanges often begin with a question (Are you well? Did you eat?), and rarely include a "hello" equivalent. Personal questioning upon meeting is typical, as a means of determining rank. Nonverbal communication trumps the spoken word.
- The idea of "face" and saving face is of high importance. Reluctancy to act is common as a way of avoiding failure or judgment. Collectivism is prized.
- Demonstrating emotion in public is highly discouraged; visible signs of anger or upset equate to a loss of face and must be avoided at all costs. A

smile or giggle may indicate happiness or embarrassment and can signal good or bad news.

- Women maintain a significant amount of personal liberties.
- Various calendars are used, including the traditional 8-day calendar; the lunar calendar; and the westernized 7-day version.
- Gifts are often rejected, as friends do not need to provide gifts, and are rarely opened in the presence of the giver.
- Touching on the head, direct eye contact, Western-style beckoning (palm up, curled forefinger), exposed soles of the feet, and left hand use may be considered offensive.
- Confrontation is avoided at all costs. It is common to respond in agreement at all times, regardless of actual feelings or plans. Nonassertiveness is a virtue; attentiveness to others' feelings when making decisions is expected.
- Same gender physical contact is acceptable and is a sign of trusting friendship.
- Birthdays are not highly relevant, and in some cases, not known.
- Culturally, fate and luck are paramount; planning and preparation are not high priorities.
- Marigolds and carnations signify death, along with the colors green, black, and blue.
- Red connotes China, which may or may not be welcome. White is a color of mourning.

Tanzania, Congo, Ghana, Nigeria, Burundi, Rwanda, Cote d' Ivore

- Family, including extended family, is the focal point of all life activity and planning. Often, the mother's brother, rather than the husband, has the most prominent influence and say in family affairs.
- Lowered gaze when conversing with a person of respect is considered polite. Elders, including nonfamily members, may be addressed as "mama," "Mzee," "aunt," or "uncle."
- Rushing a greeting without extensive conversation and inquiry is extremely rude.
- Handshakes are the common greeting; rural women may also exchange greetings with a clap and slight bow. Practising Muslims might avoid physical greetings with the opposite sex.
- Hand motions are utilized in nearly every element of speech. Specific hand signals carry direct meaning.
- Constant eye contact may create discomfort and may be regarded as impolite, especially in dealing with elders or superiors.
- Private space is not highly protected; touching and close proximity, even with strangers, is the norm.

- The left hand is usually considered unclean. Food is eaten with the fingers of the right hand. The eldest adult may serve others using both hands. Drinking during meals may be considered impolite and is usually reserved for after eating. Certain animals, which may be regarded as specific family totems, may be forbidden as food sources.
- Louder speaking tones may be the norm. However, directness in speech is not commonly practiced; answering may involve storytelling or general avoidance.
- Time and scheduling are not of high priority.
- Active storytelling, through song, dance, and oration is paramount to cultural integrity. Expressing feelings, to any degree, is socially normative, and often encouraged.
- Gender divisions may be apparent.
- Photography, especially of human subjects, may not be appreciated, or even tolerated.

Somalia, Eritrea, Ethiopia

- Immediate and extended family is the primary foundation of life. Clan affiliation is central to one's identity.
- Greetings are formal and courteous, and usually occur with a light handshake and direct eye contact; three kisses may be exchanged once familiarity has been established. Males should wait for a female to extend her hand before initiating contact. Elders should always be greeted first.
- Hand motions are utilized in nearly every element of speech. Specific hand signals carry direct meaning.
- Traditional gender roles are heavily enforced. Female children are often parented in a strict fashion; male counterparts may be allowed greater freedom.
- Gifts are to be received with both hands or the right hand alone, and are not opened at the time of receipt.
- Punctuality is not strictly enforced, but extreme lateness is considered rude.
- Shoes may need to be removed before entering a home.
- Eating should occur with the right hand only.
- When visiting a home, it is expected that coffee will be served, and it is impolite to refuse.
- All art traditions, including oral history and spoken word are part of the cultural fabric. (Somalia, in fact, is regarded as a "Nation of Poets").
- In many regions, Islam plays an integral role in all aspects of societal functioning. In these contexts, females should be covered above the ankle and wrist, and over the head, as a gesture of modesty, humility, and devotion.

Male dress incorporates Western-style clothes, cloth tied at the waist in long skirt fashion, or the traditional Arabic Khamis.

- Henna body and nail painting is an imbedded aspect of life for both genders, and especially for females.
- Westernized "thumbs up," beckoning with the forefinger, exposing the soles of the feet, and touching on the head are considered offensive behaviors.

Ecuador, Guatemala, Chile, Venezuela, Columbia, Mexico

- Family is central to social function. Loyalty to the family unit is paramount, and independent decisions are rooted in a whole-group effect. Personal relationships are the basis of business and social activity.
- First names are generally reserved for close friends and family.
- Greetings are warm and may be accompanied by handshake, or with light kisses or forearm touching for close acquaintances. Women may tap each other's forearms as a substitute for shaking hands.
- Catholicism plays a vital role in social functioning.
- Close speaking proximity with physical contact is the norm; backing away during conversation is rude. Eye contact is very important; sustained eye contact is considered polite and respectful.
- A reversed wave, with the palm of the hand turned in hand turned in, waving the self, is a means of waving goodbye.
- Loud voices in public are discouraged.
- Time is valued, but not strictly adhered to. Relationships and interpersonal connections generally override timeliness.
- Hands on hips, hands in pockets, yawning, and gum chewing while speaking are considered impolite.
- The "fig" (thumb between fisted middle and index fingers) and the "ok" signs are considered obscene.
- A girl's fifteenth birthday is a time of considerable celebration.
- Black and purple are often avoided as shades of mourning. Lilies, white flowers, and marigolds are associated with funerals.
- Certain communities may be sensitive to a right fist raised above shoulder height, a mark of Communism.
- Gifts are opened when received.
- Art in all forms is of high cultural value.

India, Nepal, Bhutan, Tibet

- Social hierarchy dominates every arena of life and interpersonal interaction. Professional titles are important.
- Family and extended family create the basis for all activity and goal setting.

- Greetings usually involve a slight bow with hands in the prayer position. The expression Namaste (Namaskar), which means "the Light in me honors the Light in you," is commonly used as a formal and informal greeting and goodbye. Handshakes or kisses may also be exchanged, but physical contact between genders may not be welcomed.
- The Western "hello" wave may be interpreted as "no," or "go away."
- A smile while quickly pulling the head back indicates "yes." Moving the head in a figure eight has a similar meaning.
- When leaving a group, it is polite to address each individual separately.
- Pointing with the forefinger is very rude. The gesture can be made with the chin or whole hand.
- Modest dress is the norm. Dressing nicely, when possible, is encouraged.
- Any form of "no" may be avoided. It is considered impolite to refuse a person his or her wishes. It is considered proper manners (and not an act of dishonesty) to be agreeable at all costs, even if the aim is not actually intended.
- Touching the head or touching another person with the feet is considered taboo. Touching or passing should only occur with the right hand.
- All names are indicative of family and religion. "Singh" indicates Sikh roots. Muslim names do not include a surname and use connectors such as "bin" or "binti" (son/daughter of) to attach the father's first name to the child's first name. Hindus may also use the father's name ahead of their first name, or may have a first name and surname.
- Generosity and gift giving are thought to enhance life and the afterlife.
- Gifts are given with both hands and are usually not opened when received. Gifts made of leather are inappropriate for Hindus. White flowers should be avoided, as they are associated with funerals.
- Shoes should be removed before entering a home.
- Eating is often done with the fingers, but only of the right hand. Knives are rarely used as utensils. Seating order is important and will be determined by the host. Leaving some food on the plate is considered polite.
- The first offer of coffee or tea should be refused out of politeness; the second should be accepted.
- Hindus and Sikhs do not eat beef, and many are vegetarian. Muslims do not consume pork.

China, Korea, Vietnam

- Family is the foundation for life. Maintaining family honor is imperative. Ancestry may be directly traced across thousands of years via male relatives. Fathers are responsible for the family; eldest sons also carry special duties and responsibilities to the family.

- Traditionally, names are recorded with the family name first, and then the middle name, and the first name last.
- A bow serves as the traditional greeting; a handshake may be used afterward. The individual of lower status will bow to the more esteemed counterpart; the most senior will prompt the handshake. Elders are always greeted first. Individuals may applaud when meeting someone or when someone new or respected enters a room.
- One should wait to be introduced in a common gathering. Indirect eye contact is a sign of respect.
- Punctuality is valued.
- Saving "face," or "kibun," is an unfailing priority. Great efforts will be taken to maintain honor and dignity for the self and the family name. Silence can be common, as a means of saving face. Spoken word and keeping promises are very important.
- Collectivism is paramount. There exists a need to be a part of a whole; independence is not valued as in the Western sense.
- Harmony is stressed, and conflict avoided. Therefore, much is expressed through nonverbal communication.
- Clocks, handkerchiefs, straw sandals, and the colors white, blue and black are ominous; they are symbolic of death. Green, white, and black are considered misfortunate, as is writing in red ink. Four is an unlucky number. Giving items in fours should be avoided.
- Gifts are presented and received with two hands and are not opened when received.
- Shoes should always be removed before entering a home.
- Dining usually involves a strict protocol, including seating and the order in which people are served and eat.
- Pointing with the finger is rude; the whole hand should be used instead. Similarly, it is offensive to stand with hands on hips, to touch someone's head or shoulder, or pass anything over the head.
- Opposite genders should not touch, unless the female initiates contact.

Belarus, Bosnia and Herzegovina, Uzbekistan, Tajikistan

- Family and familial obligations are the groundwork of social function. Motherhood is highly valued; it is not uncommon for women to marry or bear children in their mid-to-late teen years. Respect for elders is paramount.
- Introductions are warm, but overt friendliness with strangers is uncommon. Greetings may involve a simple nod and hello; handshakes and/or forearm embraces, or three exchanged kisses are also common. A very slight bow with a hand over the heart is a signal of utmost respect.

- Eye contact is expected, but is often less direct between genders.
- Timeliness is a virtue; punctuality is assumed.
- Education has a high value and is skill/task oriented.
- Personal space is not usually guarded; discomfort in close-proximity settings may be interpreted as mistrust or insult.
- Shoes should be removed before entering a home or place of stay.
- Conservative dress is the norm.
- Speaking volume norms may be higher than in the West. Straightforwardness is normative.
- Hospitality is prized and taken seriously. Offerings made in the home should be accepted; refusing food or drink may be an offense. As a host, it is considered rude to fill a cup more than half-full; it is an indication of wanting the guest to leave.
- Pointing or calling with the forefinger is rude; use of the middle finger is offensive. Showing or indicating with the first three fingers together should be strictly avoided; it is a sign of Serbian victory and may not be welcomed.
- The westernized "ok" sign is considered offensive; whistling indoors is considered bad luck.
- Spitting in public can be normative and is not considered offensive.
- Hands in the pockets while standing or conversing is considered impolite. Such is the case for sitting with legs spread apart and/or placing feet on chairs or tables.
- Flowers, given in even numbers in quantities under a dozen, may be equated with death or funerals.

Cultural Nuances Credits[6–10]

There it is: a super-abbreviated launch pad for cultural insight. These insights are not intended to function as exact or comprehensive customary explanations. The hope, however, is that they provide a generalized framework for conversation, awareness, and positive multicultural interaction. Perhaps these new frames of cultural reference will inspire additional research and investigation regarding the customs that are uniquely relevant to our individual classrooms.

The little cultural "aha's" can be tremendously beneficial to the Newcomer teaching practice. As we grow in our craft, we become more mindful of our body language, tone, gestures, and hand signals. The "ok" sign and habitual finger pointing methods of communication become points of contention. We learn to exercise cognizance when patting children on the head, pointing the soles of our shoes toward others, opening gifts given by students, and greeting parents in appropriate ways.

We may also model increased tolerance and understanding of particular student behaviors. Yari, from Mali, stands erect each time she responds to an oral prompt; this is customary according to her previous school experience. To indicate a question, Tooraj cups a hand under the opposite elbow and shoots his pointer finger straight into the air; this is expected in his native Tajikistan. *Most* of our students have trouble keeping shoes on their little feet; but most are extremely accustomed to removing them when indoors.

By cultivating our own mindfulness of the cultural distinctions that exist in our classrooms and schools, we can enjoy more meaningful and impacting relationships with our students and their families. As a holistic outcome of cultural tolerance, trust can be established. From a place of trust, we can wholly access our students' learning capabilities. This is the place where magic happens.

NOTES

1. Virtue, David C. (2009). *Serving the Needs of Immigrant and Refugee Adolescents.* Principal, VA. Vol. 89, No. 1, 64–65 S/O

2. Moore, Dennis (2004). Conceptual Policy Issues. In R. Hamilton & D. Moore (Eds.), *Educational Interventions for Refugee Children* (p. 93). London: RoutledgeFalmer.

3. Loewen, Shawn (2004). Second Language Concerns for Refugee Children. In R. Hamilton & D. Moore (Eds.), *Educational Interventions for Refugee Children* (pp. 35–52). London: RoutledgeFalmer.

4. Ferfolja, T. & Margaret Vickers (2010). Supporting Refugee Students in School Education in Greater Western Sydney. School of Education, University of Western Sydney, *Critical Studies in Education*, Vol. 51, No. 2, 149–62.

5. Charny, Joel (2008). *World Refugee Day: Where are the World's Hidden Refugees?* Refugees International. Located at www.refugeesinternational.org/blog/world-refugee-day-where-are-the-worlds-hidden-refugees. Retrieved Feb. 2014.

6. Meyer, Erin (2014). *The Culture Map: Breaking Through the Invisible Boundaries of Global Business.* PublicAffairs Publishing.

7. Morrison, Terry & Wayne A. Conaway (2006). *Kiss, Bow, or Shake Hands,* Adams Media.

8. Lustig, Myron W. & Jolene Koester (2009). *International Competence: Interpersonal Communication Across Cultures* (6th Edition). Pearson Publishing.

9. Lewis, Richard D. (2005). *When Cultures Collide: Leading Across Cultures* (3rd Edition). Nicholas Brealey Publishing.

10. Storti, Craig (2007). *The Art of Crossing Cultures* (2nd Edition). International Press.

Unit II

INTO THE CLASSROOM

Chapter 6

The Language Piece

Danışıq Dili -Azerbaijani

ORAL LANGUAGE: THE VOICE OF BELONGING

Language shapes how we think, and the influx of recent immigrants from hundreds of linguistic backgrounds presents a unique challenge to American schools.[1]

Oral language is very often the centerpiece of cultural cohesiveness, as it makes communication possible. Communication, meanwhile, is the foundation of human interconnectedness. Beyond allowing for the rituals of communal exchange, oral language is the primary platform upon which creative expression and universal sense making are constructed. It tells the story of the beginning, the end, and everything in between. It relates the family tree, defines social norms, solidifies romance, and generates war. Our world is made up of *words*.

All cultures demonstrate a high degree of oral reliance.[2] In certain regions, the communicative aspects of a culture permeate and sustain every grain of social function. In fact, most non-Western languages are rooted heavily in oral tradition. Many cultures are far more reliant upon verbal output and body language than printed text as a means of communicative exchange. Many of our new-to-English students come from these rich oral-centric backgrounds.

In much of Africa, for example, it is common for an individual to demonstrate agility in multiple local and national tongues, even when literacy abilities are restricted. In communities where legal contracts can be accomplished with a verbal handshake, print concepts may be extraneous to successful daily living. Of course, we understand that literacy is nonnegotiable for our students. Still, it may be helpful to understand the utter potency and significance of oral language in the Newcomer setting.

FINDING BALANCE: SUPPORTING HOST-LANGUAGE GROWTH AND HERITAGE LANGUAGE PRESERVATION

The ultimate goal of the Newcomer framework is to facilitate English language learning at an accelerated rate, and to prepare students for continued mainstream scholastic and post-school successes. As previously mentioned, one of the best courses of action that we can take in enhancing host language development is to outspokenly value and actively encourage heritage language preservation. While this may seem counterintuitive, research continues to illuminate the benefits of this practice.[3]

The most significant reasons for heritage language preservation have to do with maintaining a coherent self-identity.[4] Moreover, native language acts as a tie that unites families and ethnic communities. When this tie is severed, a sense of belonging is compromised.

A majority of ELLs who are successful in maintaining heritage and host languages also perform better academically than ELLs who are restricted to host language learning at the expense of heritage language.[5] This trend has been documented in standardized testing, as well as in ACTs and SATs. Bilingualism impacts the brain in profound ways, enhancing cognitive function and long-term memory (including the proven delay of dementia and Alzheimer's disease).[6]

Dual-language skills also enrich problem-solving abilities, promote flexibility and multitasking abilities, and provide for future opportunities with regard to college learning and beyond.[7]

Meanwhile, valuing heritage languages in the classroom encourages tolerance, global awareness, and belonging. Maintaining the host language can also expedite host language acquisition.[8,9] Shawn Loewen writes: "It is important for second language children to feel that their first language and culture are valued and respected. It is particularly important for refugee children . . . to use their first language with other children, their teachers, and at home."[10]

In the classroom context, we can enable heritage language preservation by allowing our students periods of time where they are encouraged to communicate with linguistically similar students, where applicable, for a short period, and repeating out thoughts in English. We can provide texts representing a variety of cultures and/or languages (see chapter 8 for a multicultural reading list), and we can relay to parents, through a translator when necessary, the importance of maintaining heritage language skills in the home. Through and because of first language fluency, second (or third) language efficacy is more likely to occur.

"WE KNOW WE'VE DONE A GREAT JOB WHEN . . ."

Language Learning Objectives

The foundational goal of ELA-E instruction is to promote and advance English language speaking, reading, and writing abilities across a range of social and content areas. In our day-to-day instruction, we accomplish this task through language learning objectives. So what exactly are language learning objectives?

Simply, *content language objectives define and/or clarify the language necessary to meet the learning goal, or content objective.* When we refer to *language learning objectives*, we are asking the following essential questions:

- What is the function of language in the given (content area) context?
- What language structures are required to achieve the language function?
- What are the prominent concepts of the lesson?
- What key vocabulary words are associated with the context learning?
- What is the current level of students' speech and understanding?

Essentially, students' deep knowledge acquisition is codependent on a terrific number of language variables. First, learners are expected to produce functional efficacy (e.g., basic conversational skills, direction following skills,) in the instructional language. In our case, that is English. If this prerequisite is unmet, students will experience difficulty in navigating basic elements of communication.

In the classroom setting, these basic skills allow students to understand their task and ask for clarification. That is, the language piece facilitates authentic participation. If students do not recognize the core of the lesson— that is, *what they are being asked to perform, recognize, or anticipate*—the lesson is lost. If students are further unable to communicate a need for assistance or elucidation, then our instructional agenda becomes a futile endeavor. We fail our students.

Second, students must demonstrate *content language* understanding. We refer to this as academic language, and it is the essence of our craft. In teacher talk, this sounds like: *identify the noun; name the prism; describe the setting; or predict the volume.* If students are deficient in the tools necessary to comprehend basic conversational language in school, then they cannot be prepared to access and apply academic language. Furthermore, if learners and instructors are without a common ground in academic language, how can we possibly anticipate or accelerate student successes?

Essentially, content learning/language objectives (CLOs) follow a general pattern. They present a language-related function and outcome for a given subject. Here are a few templates that may be of use. The phrase "in complete sentences" is frequently used, with intent. This end cap covers essential elements of the language objective. Meanwhile, speaking in complete sentences is a fundamental skill for Newcomers, and all students.

Remember, language functions are tools or mechanisms that are used for oral expression. Examples of language functions include: retell, explain, talk about, describe, compare, contrast, ask about, suggest, persuade, sequence, convince, name, and state an opinion. Students should be able to relay their language objective throughout the lesson. Below are several examples for writing language objectives for ELA-E instruction.

Sample Structure

Today we are learning about _____.
We know we've done a great job when:
we can (insert academic function) (insert academic output) and we can (insert language function) (insert language output) to a friend using complete sentences.

Sample Objective 1:

Today we are learning about multiplication.
We know we've done a great job when:
we can (multiply) (single digit numbers to 100) and we can (describe) (our problem-solving strategy) to a friend using complete sentences.

Sample Objective 2:

Today we are learning about our solar system.
We know we've done a great job when:
we can (identify) (the sun and the eight planets in our solar system) and we can (explain) (our reasoning) to a friend using complete sentences.

Sample Objective 3:

Today we are learning about capitalization.
We know we've done a great job when:
we can (correctly use) (capital letters in our writing) and we can (tell a friend) (three different times or ways to use a capital letter), using complete sentences.

GET THE MOTOR RUNNING: COOPERATIVE LEARNING STRUCTURES

Our first charge as Newcomer educators is to *get the words out*. We want to know who our learners are. We hope to understand their thoughts and goals, and we need to know how to best service them. Cooperative Learning Structures are an effective means of acquiring and practicing new language skills across a range of settings and demographics. Essentially, cooperative structures are avenues for learning in which participants directly engage with each other in meaningful, constructive, strategically guided ways.

Cooperative learning calls for academic verbal exchange that occurs with purpose and productivity, and enhances the learning experience through accountability. Cooperative learning processes are guided, with scaffolds in place. They are also designed to be practiced with continuity, such that participants eventually self-promote the objective behaviors and language structures.[11]

A key facet of cooperative learning is its reliance upon participants' thoughtful attentiveness and engaged effort as they respond to rigorous prompts with clarity and intentionality. In the shared cooperative space, each contributor's thoughts are valid and relevant. Each response is an opportunity for students to experience growth and development as active host language speakers and listeners.

Another advantage to cooperative language engagement is that it is wholly cross-curricular; and it is unrestricted by subject, genre, or student population. Cooperative structures have a beneficial place in scientific inquiry, social studies discourse, beginning English introductions, team-building exercises, explanation of learning, and concept elaboration, among others. Applied appropriately, cooperative learning is a best practices approach to ELA instruction.

Hundreds of cooperative learning structures exist, each with the goal of structured, meaningful talk in mind.[12,13] Here are some great starters for the classroom or any intentional-conversation context:

Partner-Pair-Share: In this exercise, designed by Frank Lyman (1981), students receive information from the facilitator, think about the input information, talk with a peer or "elbow mate" about their thoughts using cooperative talk stems (see cooperative structures), and present pair ideas.

Inside-Outside Circle: A group of students forms a small circle and faces outward. The rest of the students form an outside circle, looking inward at one partner. Facilitator asks either the inside or outside circle to share a specific idea or thought with the partner. Facilitator cues change: inside circle remains in place, while outside circle shifts one place to the right, forming a new partnership. Then the process repeats.

Fish Bowl: A small group of learners meets in the center of the room. Other students sit around the small group. Learners in the small group engage in structured cooperative discussion, while the outside group observes and takes notes on the inner group's conversation. Afterwards, observing students can share their thoughts and contributions. Then the roles reverse.

Four Corners: The four corners of a room are labeled: *agree, strongly agree, disagree, and strongly disagree.* Learners are asked a series of questions, either personal or academic. Participants move to the quadrant that they align with. They may be encouraged to share thoughts with others in their corner or with the class as a whole.

Numbered Heads: Students are placed in teams of 3–5. Each student within a group is numbered 1–5. Facilitator calls out a number for the round (e.g. 2). Teams will be called upon to answer a question. Whole groups will talk and work the problem out together; however, the specified "numbered head" will be responsible for reporting the team's answer. This approach is very helpful in supporting beginning language learners in building confidence, fluency, and trust.

Line-Ups: This process works much in the same way as inside-outside circle, but in straight lines. Students form two lines and face each other. Students respond to prompts using cooperative supports. To rotate, one line remains immobile, while the first person from the other line moves to the end of that line, and other students move up. The process is repeated with new partners.

Jigsaw: Groups of students are responsible for researching and reporting on one aspect of a topic. Each group presents, such that an entire topic is addressed via cooperative student talk.

SHELTERED INSTRUCTION FOR COOPERATIVE TALK

For beginning Newcomers, and even advanced language students, it is a good idea to provide participants with sentence stem starters. Sentence stems provide opportunities for ELLs to successfully participate in classroom activities in structured, purposeful ways. Stems can be used to scaffold both oral and written expression. Here, we will concentrate on sentence stems for oral language development.

With regard to early learners, one or two options are plenty. With students' progression, the range and complexity of cooperative structure prompts can be expanded correspondingly. Sentence stems should be visible while a student is speaking, and should be modeled and practiced leading up to independent production. Accomplished sentence stems are additionally helpful when posted as daily classroom anchor charts. Below is a basic collection of oral language production stems.

Table 6.1 Cooperative Talk: Speaking and Listening Cues

As a Speaker I can Say/Ask . . .	
I think that . . .	Did you notice that . . .
This reminds me of . . .	I am picturing/I predict that . . .
In my opinion . . .	I understand, but . . .
I was surprised that . . .	I discovered that . . .
I liked/disliked when . . .	I hope that/wonder if . . .

Table 6.2 As a Listener I Can Say/Ask . . .

Can you explain?	I am unclear about . . .
I agree/disagree about . . .	I was confused when . . .
Can you show me?	Would you give an example?
Could you tell me more?	How did you discover that?
Could that also mean that . . .	Or maybe . . .

THE POWER OF VISUAL CUES

Most individuals, in most circumstances, will employ sight as the first sensual resource when encountering something new or unexpected. In a similar regard, Newcomer students will rely heavily on visual stimuli in order to comprehend and make sense of their new surroundings. Visual stimulation can grant access to areas that are familiar, recognizable, and safe; and with safety, learning is possible.

In the preliminary stages of relocation, Newcomers absorb and digest the visual impact of their new surroundings in a heightened way, namely because the language comprehension piece is compromised. Meanwhile, the Newcomer brain is busy at work, processing very physical comparisons between the home and host environment.

A tendency exists for Newcomers to hone in on any apparent similarities and cling to them. Through identified elements of similarity, an individual is able to establish connections between home and host languages. Here, new language exploration occurs.

In the classroom setting, linguistic openness also opens doors and windows for relationship building. It might sound like this: "*Miss . . . do you know, in my country, we call this thing 'book': kitabe/sah-oh/leai.*" Interestingly, book is *kitab* in Swahili, Arabic, Turkish and Nepali—and so now social connections are created!

Picture dictionaries offer another practical use for visual cuing. Use of this tool should be explicitly modeled, and learners should enjoy unobstructed access to dictionaries and glossaries, especially illustrated versions. This can easily be incorporated as an integral part of daily, second-nature practice! Letter identification, alphabetizing, and word-sleuthing are all functional

As a mechanism of visual cuing, **icons** should be an integral part of any Newcomer or ELL classroom and school. For example, a door might have a tag on it, with the picture of a door, along with the corresponding English print, d-o-o-r . A girls' bathroom door might have the face of a g-i-r-l . The American f-l-a-g will be labeled the same way, along with the p-e-n-c-i-l drawer, and b-o-o-k shelf.

elements of vocabulary expansion. Meanwhile, occasions for students to practice self-reliance and open literary exploration promote confidence, self-esteem, and overall academic efficacy.

VOCABULARY BUILDERS

"Call and Response: Call-and-response is a standard form of leader-to-group communication in many non-Western cultures and may be employed as an effective teaching/learning tool. In these exercises, the leader (noting that a student can also act as leader) will call out, and the responders will echo with a known riposte. African call-and-respond chants such as "Jambo" or "Kye Kye Kule" are great places to start. These exchanges can be used to gain students' attention and to practice oral fluency, intonation and other skills.

Word Exchange: Present half of the class with new vocabulary words written on index cards. Then, distribute definitions cards to the remaining children. Encourage students to interact, exchange ideas, and problem solve to match each new word with its corresponding definition. For added linguistic practice, allow each pair an opportunity to present their word set to the class. If time allows, partners may compose and display labeled drawings, charts (such as the Frayer model, presented graphic organizers), songs or skits to explain the target word.

Editors-in-Chief: Provide students with opportunities to edit proper and improper English audio and text. This tactic helps students as they learn to decide what "sounds right" or "looks right" in customary and academic English. Such exercises are an opportunity to express competency at multiple levels of English expertise, thus encouraging students' linguistic esteem and self-confidence.

Label Makers: Utilize labeling as an effective technique for vocabulary and language development. Labeling provides a tiered level of active participation and encourages engagement and self-esteem at multiple levels of English development. For example, using a picture of a farm, allow students to utilize English in labeling as many items from the scene as possible. This is a valuable exercise in working with academic language and sentence building.

Dictionaries: As an expansion activity, students can take ownership in creating and maintaining their own picture/definition dictionaries. Students draw a picture in the corresponding letter frame of their dictionary and work to compose an appropriate definition. They may also record a word and transfer a glossary definition into their personal dictionaries for future reference. Whole class dictionaries and personal dictionaries are both effective.

At the beginning of each year, it surprises me to see how much students struggle with personal dictionaries. A few short months later, most children complete tasks with little guidance. By mid-year, even very young and/or beginning level students are comfortably exploring the deeper nature of alphabetizing; for example, use of third-and-fourth letter guideposts (i.e., condensation, condescend, comfortable, compound).

Word Strength: Guide students in the process of ordering feeling words from the least to the most exaggerated meaning. For example: sad, depressed; glad, happy, elated; eager, impatient, anxious; awake, energetic, wild. This activity can be accomplished using number line scales or other visual cues. For an expanded table of emotions, see below.

Tongue Twisters: Invite students to provide examples of tongue twisters in the home language. If they do not know any, use this opportunity as a chance for learners to enlist their parents' help as a homework assignment.

Table 6.3 Emotion Words

Happy	Sad	Angry	Excited	Glad
Generous	Hurt	Alone	Tired	Surprised
Energetic	Helpful	Guilty	Lonely	Curious
Disappointed	Confident	Kind	Restless	Sorry
Brave	Calm	Important	Loving	Annoyed
Anxious	Cheerful	Amazed	Different	Afraid
Lucky	Safe	Threatened	Wonderful	Sleepy
Interested	Confident	Humiliated	Abandoned	Eager
Free	Suspicious	Upset	Enthusiastic	Appreciated
Frustrated	Aggressive	Nosy	Hopeful	Playful
Quiet	Uneasy	Panicked	Insecure	Delighted
Fortunate	Comfortable	Overwhelmed	Disgusted	Pleased
Scared	Satisfied	Heartbroken	Shy	Fascinated
Tearful	Capable	Abandoned	Daring	Tense
Frightened	Unsure	Proud	Determined	Left-out
Ashamed	Clever	Anxious	Startled	Jealous
Shocked	Inspired	Respected	Great	Loved
Included	Appreciative	Relaxed	Understanding	Smart
Disappointed	Interested	Thrilled	Sorrowful	Bad
Uneasy	Thankful	Exhausted	Confused	Loving
Famished	Amused	Irritated	Curious	Proud
Supportive	Narcissistic	Obnoxious	Hurtful	Bitter
Social	Jolly	Festive	Evil	Serene

Table 6.4   Basic Tongue Twister Template

Proper noun	*OR*	Who?
Verb		What?
Location		Where?
Time		When?
Reason		Why?

Allow children to share and exchange their native tongue twisters. As a writing assignment, have students transcribe the meaning of their home-language tongue twisters into English. This is an excellent time to practice phonics, and also to make use of dictionaries, glossaries, web-based translators and other linguistic-exchange tools that might be available in the classroom.

An abbreviated listing of international tongue twisters is available in the appendices.

In the meantime, you can have plenty of fun creating your own tongue twisters! For a few simple formulas to use with alliteration (repeated first letter), see Table 6.4

Students may also work in collaborative groups to say and write tongue twisters. In this case, the first student is responsible for the "who," and the second for the "why," and so on. Compiled tongue twisters also make for excellent classroom publications!

Descriptive Pairs: This exercise can be used to review and practice previously learned vocabulary. To begin, one student faces the playing board, while the partnering student turns away. The child who is viewing the content will use as many English words as possible to aid their partner in guessing the target word. The facilitating student may describe what something looks like, sounds like, feels like, tastes like, smells like, or is similar to; but he or she is not allowed to speak the target word at any time. Pairs of students keep points for the number of correct solutions. Partners reverse, vocabulary banks are renewed, and student pairs work to surpass their preceding score. A sample board game follows.

Object-Verb Match: Learners who are new to the English language show opportunities for growth in specific areas, including pronoun distinction, tense markers, and object-verb agreement. Object-verb match activities are simple and provide opportunities for vocabulary expansion on a range of skill and participatory levels.

Object-verb matches work especially well in accountable-talk scenarios, such as numbered heads, inside/outside, or pair share. The idea may also be adapted to complement recorded brainstorming sessions (individually, in pairs, in groups or as a class). With practice, students will become able to create meaningful subject-action connections with relative ease and

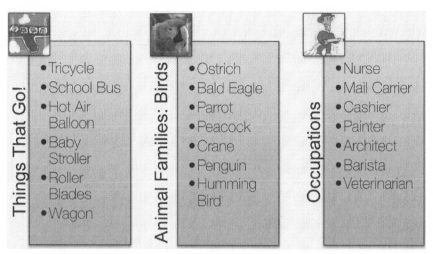

Figure 6.3 Descriptive Pairs Template

maneuverability. Ultimately, learners will establish familiarity with target word sets, which, in turn, become the foundation for accurate sentence construction.

A typical object-verb activity might look something like this:

LESSON: Using sticky notes, post three to five nouns at various locations in the classroom. Visual imagery—magazine pictures, stuffed animals, or stickers—may be attached to the noun examples. Invite students to identify as many corresponding verbs as possible for each noun provided. For example, a clipping of a scientist excavating a fossil might generate: *search (ing), dig, look, think, brush, walk, label, study, name, write/record, travel, talk, save/ preserve, protect, carry, store.* Allow students the opportunity to share their thoughts with other learners (Inside-Outside circles and acting out work wonderfully!). For example:

- *Pencil:* write, draw, twirl, tap, erase, break, sharpen, scribble, print, shade
- *Computer:* print, copy, type, search, download, play, edit, file, save
- *Towel:* wipe, dry, clean, mop, wring, wash, dry, hang, use, share, spread

Word Relays: Students work in teams of 3–6. Each team moves to a corner of the room. Place a pile of content/unit-specific words in the center of the room. Next to the content words, place a second pile of combined conjunctions, prepositions, punctuation marks, and "double underline" cards (to indicate use of capital letters). Single representatives from each team select one word and return to his or her "base." This process will continue until one of

Yesterday afternoon	I she he they I you all it we you	played ate skipped they rode discovered drew ran sang climbed	hopscotch on the playground. four slices of pizza. all the way to California. in an airplane. a hidden treasure. pictures of dinosaurs. right after me! a song from Burma. the tallest building on Earth!

Figure 6.4   Sentence Frame Table

the teams successfully arranges collected words into a meaningful, correctly ordered sentence.

Sentence Frames: See Cooperative Structures. Example: Desert places are _____ and _____. Sentence stems can be more formatted, but with room for participant choice. In this case, sheltered instruction for sentence formulation would follow a template similar to the example given in Figure 6.4.

EVERY LEARNER, A STORY TO TELL

Human lives are elaborate conglomerations of *new* things. We become accustomed to certain people, places, and events over time; they become less new to us. Eventually, we may even realize *ownership* of these experiences; they become our reality, an element of our self-composition.

Storytelling can be a very valid means to experiment with the new language in a variety of contexts. It is an accessible option at various stages of the language acquisition process, and it is a skill that can develop in accordance with a learner's expanding linguistic capabilities. Also, storytelling is a versatile practice with cross-curricular value. Storytelling can be engaging and entertaining, as most children are enamored with the magical "I." In the storytelling element, there is opportunity to relish in the self-story and to share select pieces of it at a comfortable pace in a safe classroom environment.

There is an additional dimension to storytelling that can be profoundly cathartic and healing. The particular exercise of capturing human feelings and experiences, through fictional characters or biographical ones, allows students opportunities to release, revisit, question, and make sense of poignant life events. The retelling of personal experiences creates a fertile ground for self-discovery and social understanding.

Storytelling isn't always pretty, or graceful, or dynamic. Under the right conditions, however, storytelling *can* reveal much about a student's personality and life view. This phenomenon can occur, even in the earliest stages of host language introduction. Storytelling can be a great way to stimulate students' oral and written expression. Additionally, storytelling can function as a summative assessment tool for language proficiency and reading comprehension.[14]

As one means of incorporating storytelling into classroom protocol, ELD specialist Lia Ridley recommends inviting students to assemble a small box of meaningful items, and to share about selected artifacts. Students are often very curious to learn about each other's lives and respective cultures. Interestingly, participants routinely recognize many more commonalities among each other than differences. However, these differences, (language, dress, and custom, for example) can become highlights of a child's native country in very positive ways.

One of my favorite storytelling (and writing) topics involves . . . teeth! I learned early in my career that the Tooth Fairy is a very West-centric element of culture. Further, I became fascinated to discover that my students' lost-tooth traditions were very different from my own and from other peers!

Some cultures toss a lost tooth on the roof with a prayer to Condor. Others toss the tooth backward between the legs, or over their heads. Some bury it in the ground in the hopes that it will manifest into a chicken; and still other traditions involve mice, rats, ladders, and a "tooth store where they pull out my tooth with a tool and give my mom a check to keep my tooth." Indeed, this is an opportunity for storytelling expression.

I like to add lined tooth template paper, a dental hygiene mini book, and a pile of toothbrushes to give away. We also add an in-class demonstration

Table 6.5 Storytelling Topics

When I was _ years old . . .	My school/ class/ friends/ teacher . . .	My family members . . .
A story I hear/was told . . .	A tradition in my family . . .	My favorite holiday . . .
My friend . . .	A traditional song/ poem/ story . . .	I am happy/ sad/ afraid because/ when . . .
I remember . . .	When I grow up . . .	My contribution to the world . . .
In my country . . .	When I first came to America . . .	What I love/ miss about . . .
Something I like to do/think about/eat . . .	In my language/ culture . . .	I feel important because/ when . . .

Credit: Lia Ridley, ELA-E Specialist (5)

Figure 6.5

and practice of tooth brushing, and some mirror aided "Smile Portraits." This makes for an entertaining interactive unit overflowing with fresh vocabulary opportunities and content learning applications!

There are so *many* creative venues for storytelling. Table 6.5 gives some terrific introductory prompts.[15] As students become more fluid with their words, they are able to add depth and intricacy to their storytelling. Every child *does* have a story to tell. Each one is brilliant; and every one ripens at his or her own miraculous time.

FINDING THE BRANCHES: CELEBRATING THE FAMILY TREE

Teachers know very well the critical impact of a child's home life on his or her scholastic success. We are also cognizant of the family's larger effect upon a child's emotional, mental, and cognitive well-being. In many cases— at least from the students' vantage—we are walking, breathing buffer zones between the worlds of school and home.

As one means of bridging home and family, students may be prompted to record family trees (in English or native language script). Opportunities to record personal and relevant information can be highly motivating. By incorporating the native language piece, Newcomer students can share about themselves in ways that lend to a positive classroom culture. Most importantly, constructing a family tree can generate strong vocabulary connections for English words like *mother, brother, aunt,* and *cousin.*

Figure 6.5 shows one template for personal identification and family sharing.

HERITAGE REPORTS

Heritage reports are designed to guide students in expressing their personal stories with others via sheltered instruction. The exercise also enhances meaningful vocabulary expansion. Finally, heritage reports are a fascinating means of promoting positive classroom culture and fostering healthy, tolerant school-based relationships.

Ultimately, heritage reports or heritage "books" act as venues for conversational interaction. As a culminating activity, as a class project, authors may choose to operate a "Heritage Booth" in a communal area of the school. Other classes can sign up to visit the heritage booth and engage with our class about their compositions.

Heritage authors are usually very eager to document, show, and share their projects with an audience. Meanwhile, they are practicing cooperative language structures and cultural normative values (handshaking and simple greetings for each guest) throughout the process!

Authors routinely demonstrate an enormous sense of pride and accomplishment in sharing the final products with other faculty and students. Learners enjoy finding commonalities (*Oh, Miss—we eat this thing in my country, too!*); and they relish in the distinct curiosities of cultures different from their own. The experience allows a viable podium for respectful exchange (*So, what is the name for the cloth that the girl put on her head? Why does she have to wear it?*). It is a medium between grades, classes, and linguistic compatibility. More than all of these things, the task is educationally relevant.

To begin the heritage books, aid students in locating cultural artifacts (literature samples, photos, clothing, music, film, and parent testimony, for example). Viable sources might include the home, library, internet, community members and organizations, or international markets. Next, children will enter the writing process (of course, preliminary overview and practice with the writing process is encouraged). The following template is a generalized one, and can be adapted to suit a variety of student needs and demographics.

Note: The term "essay" in this context has open interpretation. Sheltered instruction allows for expression in a variety of ways, which may or may not incorporate organized sentence structure.

A basic Heritage Report template might include:

• Student-created cover page
• A table of contents
• Flags of native and new countries, with brief descriptions of each
• *About Me* template writing
• Family tree

All About Me

Hello! My name is _____.

I am a _____ (boy/girl). I am _____ years old.

I am from _____.

My language is _____.

Now I live in _____.

I live with _____.

My school is _____

My teacher's name is _____.

I hope you enjoyed learning about me!

All About Me

Hello! My name is _____.

I am a _____ (boy/girl). I am _____ years old.

I am from _____, and the language I speak is _____.

I came to America in _____ because _____.

I feel _____ about my new home.

I live in my house with _____.

I have _____ brothers and _____ sisters.

I am the _____ (oldest/youngest/middle) child in my family.

My new address is _____

_____

_____.

The name of my school is _____

_____.

My teacher's name is _____.

What I like most about school is _____.

Some of my new friends are named _____ , _____, and _____.

When I am not at school I like to _____.

Something very special to me is _____

because _____.

Something wonderful about me is _____.

My family is most proud of me when _____.

When I grow up I hope to _____.

I hope you enjoyed learning about me!

Chapter 6

HERITAGE FLAG REPORT

I am from _____ .

The flag of my country has these colors:

_____ . Also, the flag of my country _____   _____ .
It looks like this:

___

HERITAGE FLAG REPORT

Now I live in the United States of America.
The U.S. flag has the colors_____, _____, and _____ .
Also, my new flag has _____ stars ★ and _____ stripes ▬▬. It looks
like this:

Figure 6.9   Heritage Book Work Examples

- Traditional costume and essay
- Traditional home and essay
- Photos of family, native home, friends, or school *where possible*. (*Some students may have few or no existing photos from earlier life stages. In this case, photos from the current school year may be an excellent option.)
- Family member interviews
- Internet research with printed photos from home country, labeled
- Additional information relevant to the student and/or class unit of study
- Lyrics to traditional songs or poems

STORYTELLING THROUGH THE YEAR:
CULTURE CALENDARS

A close look at our westernized calendar reveals a prescribed exclusivity to Euro-Christian tradition. This is evidenced in the formulation of our work weeks, common holidays, school breaks. Will Kymlicka contends that "the idea that public schools may somehow be 'neutral' with respect to culture faces some rather daunting challenges, not only with respect to such basic things as language and dress code but also public holidays, and even the definition of the school week itself."[16] This truth is neither a good or bad one; it is merely a reflection of our Western history.

As Newcomer educators, however, this honest perspective is an interesting one to hold in mind. It is especially relevant as we consider the challenges that our Newcomer families might face in adjusting to life in the host setting. With such insight, we can be more open-minded to the fact that while our western calendar seems commonsensical to us, it may not seem so commonsensical to our Newcomers.

As professional educators, we promote mainstream social norms every day. In the Newcomer classroom, we carry added responsibilities: we are often our students' first line of exposure to time- and date-sensitive traditions in the host culture. While our traditional Western calendars, celebrations, and shared national agendas may not apply directly to all members of our society, they are definitive pieces of our country's composite, and essential elements of assimilation information for our Newcomers.

In our unique classroom settings, these host normative holidays *should* be explicitly taught. We can allow ourselves to be open books on the topics of Santa, the Easter Bunny, leprechauns, and thanksgiving feasts. These are novelty fascinations for many Newcomers; and also valid and inherent pieces of their new popular culture, which they will naturally be exposed to.

In a similar regard, we have a responsibility to recognize that our calendar is not the only known or acceptable framework, globally speaking. In fact, this couldn't be farther from the truth. To many, our "obvious" rhythms, patterns, and schedules of daily and annual living, are anything but obvious! It is an extraordinary thing to celebrate the immense differences in the most seemingly mundane occurrences. The calendar presents a perfect opportunity to relish in these variances.

Let's take an inventory of the "Winter Break," for instance. Which of our students are inclined to celebrate Christmas, Quaid-e-Azam, Rizal Day, Ashura, Hanukah, (or F, none of the above)? How about those days when seven Nepali students are absent at once? What's the deal with that entire section of middle school students who skip lunch and water breaks for a whole month? Or the handful of students who arrive to class the morning after the Water Festival, with their shirts and pants and shoes still damp from the celebration the night before? Or the ever mysterious mass henna and *Tan-uu-kah* face paint outbreaks?

Welcome to the wonderful, fabulous domain of the Newcomer teacher! Lucky us, we have classrooms full of pint-sized teachers, willing and enthusiastic to share their traditions and experiences with us! The question we are

january
Independence Day, Sudan; 2-Martyrdom of Imam Reza, Iran; 4-Martyrs of Independ. Day, Congo; 4-Independ. Day, Myanmar; 6-Epiphany, Columbia; 7-Coptic Christmas Day, Egypt, Ethiopia; 7-Victory Day, Cambodia; 13-Prophet Mohamed's birthday, Islamic nation; 14-Old New Year, Russia; 15-John Chilembwe Day, Malawi; 17-Thaipusam, Malaysia; 22-Unity Day, Ukraine;22-Plurinational State Foundation Day, Bolivia; 28-29-Tet holiday, Vietnam; 30-Shahid Diwas, Martyrs Day, Nepal

february
1-5-Tet holiday, Vietnam; 3-Constitution Day, Mexico; 4-Festival of Kites, Pakistan; 4-Saraswati Puja,arts festival, Nepal; 5-Kashmir Day, Pakistan; 11-Revolution Day, Iran; 14-Valentine's Day; 14-Makha Bucha, Thailand;15-Liberation Day, Afganistan; 17-Revolution Day, Libya;19-Indepen. Day, Nepal; 23-Defender of the Fatherland Day, Belarus; 24-Dragobete, Romania; 27-Independence Day, Dominican Republic

march
1-Martisor, Romania; 2-Adwa Victory Day, Ethiopia; 3-4-Carnival, Ecuador; 8-March 8 Revolution, Syria; 12-Renovation Day, Gabon;16-Fagu Purnima, Festival of Colors, Nepal; 21-Benito Juárez's Birthday Memorial, Mexico; 21-Norooz (Persian New Year); 21-23-Nauryz, Kazakhstan; 22-24-Norooz Holiday; 23-Pakistan Day; 26-Martyrs' Day, Mali; 27*-Tabaung Pwè Pagoda Festivals, Myanmar, Burma;

april
4-Independ. Day, Senegal; 6-Chakri Day, Thailand; 9-Day of Valor, Philippeans; 9-Liberation Day Iraq; 13-16-Thingyan Burmese Water Festival, New Year; 10*-Passover, Israel; 13-Navabarsha, New Year, Nepal; 15-Songkran, Thailand; 14-16-Khmer New Year, Cambodia; 14-America Day, Honduras; 17-Maundy Thursday, Ecuador; 17-Evacuation Day, Syria; 19-Landing of the 33 Patriots Day, Uruguay; 25-Sinai Liberation Day, Egypt; 28-Mujahideen Victory Day, Afghanistan; 30-Liberation Day, Vietnam;

may
6-Buddha Purnima/Vesak, Bangladesh; 9-Victory Day, Belarus; 10*-Independence Day, Israel; 14-Kamuzu Day, Malawi; 20-Whit Monday, Gabon; 22-Unity Day, Yemen; 24-Independence Day, Eritrea; 25-Africa Day, Mali; 27-Shab e-Barat, Bagladesh; 29-Ganatantra Diwas, Republic Day, Nepal

june
19-Corpus Christi, Dominican Republic; 20-Martyr's Day-Eritrea; 21-Aymara New Year Day, Bolivia; 26-Independence of State of Somaliland, Somalia; 30-Independence Day, Congo; 30-Revolution Day, Sudan

july

1-Independence Day, Somalia; 1-Independence Day, Burundi; 1-Sir Seretse Khama Day, Botswana; 3-Independence Day, Belarus; 4-Independence Day, United States; 6-Day of the Capital, Kazakhstan; 6-7-Kupalle Day, Belarus; 6-Independence Day, Malawi;14-Republic Day, Iraq; 18-Constitution Day, Uruguay; 22-Start of Buddhist Lent, Festival of Lights, Myanmar Burma; 23-Revolution Day, Egypt; 24-Night of Destiny, Bangladesh; 28-Eid-al-Fitr, Ethiopia;

august

5-Independence Day, Burkino Faso; 8-Ceasefire Day, Iraq; 15-Flooding of the Nile Observance,15-Constitution Day, Guinea; Egypt; 15-Assumption, Burkina Faso; 19-Independence Day, Afghanistan; 24-Independence Day, Ukraine; 25-Independence Day, Uruguay; 30-Victory Day, Turkey; 30-Constitution Day, Kazakhstan; 31-National Day, Malaysia;

september

2-Independence Day, Vietnam; 9-Independence Day, Tajikistan; 11-New Year, Ethiopia; 10*-Rosh Hashanah, Israel;11-Geez New Year, Eritrea; 15-Pchum Ben Festival, Cambodia; 22-Independence Day, Mali; 24-Our Lady of Las Mercedes, Dominican Republic;24-Khmer New Year, Cambodia; 25-Ghatasthapana, start of Dashain, Nepal; 25-First Revolution Day, Yemen; 30-Botswana Day;

october

1-National Day, Nigeria; 3-Morazan´s Day, Honduras; 3-Independ. Day, Iraq; 4-Eid al-Adha*, Islam; 5-Dashin Duwadashi, Nepal; 6-Oct. Liberatory War, Syria; 12-Independ. Day, Guinea; 14-2nd Revolution Day, Yemen; 19-Festval of Lights, Myanmar;21-Ndadaye Day, Burundi; 23-Diwali/Deepavali, Malyasia; 23-Peace Agreement Day, Cambodia; 23-Chulalongkorn Day, Thailand; 23-Liberation Day, Libya; 25-Islamic New Year* 25-Muharram/New Year, Malaysia; 29-Chhath Parwa, Hindi Sun God Festival, Nepal;

november

2-Deceased ones day, Uruguay; 3-Independ. of Cuenca, Ecuador; 4-Ashura*, Iran; 4-Unity Day, Russia; 6-birth of first Sikh; 7-Oct. Revolution Day, Belarus; 9-Independ. Day, Cambodia; 9-National Reconciliation Day, Tajikistan; 17-Independ. of Cartagena, Columbia; 20-Revolution Day, Mexico; 20-Water/Boat Festival*, Cambodia; 21-Dayton Peace Agreement Day, Bosnia; 30-Bonifacio Day, Philippines

december

6-Yomari punhi, end rice season, Nepal; 8-Feast of the Immaculate Conception, Columbia; 8-Constitution Day, Romania; 13-Ashura, Iran*; 16-Independ. Day, Kazakhstan; 16-Victory Day, Bangldesh; 17-National Day, Bhutan; 21-Demise of Prophet Muhammad, Iran; 23-Emperor's Birthday, Japan; 24-Independ. Day, Libya; 24-Christmas Eve; 25-Chistmas Day; 25-Quaid-e-Azam* Day, Pakistan; 25-Day of the Family, Uruguay; 30-Rizal Day, Philippines;

to ask ourselves then: how does our lesson planning and classroom talk reflect these and other celebrations?

Options for calendar exploration and connected classroom applications are virtually limitless! A modified classroom calendar is a great launch point.

Here's a quick reference list. Better yet, enlist the help of your students to carve out other important national and cultural calendar days.

Abbreviated List of Holidays throughout the World

(With a focus on countries of high refugee origination)

NOTES

1. McCracken, Janet Brown (1993). *Valuing Diversity in the Primary Years.* National Institute for the Education of the Young, Washington DC.

2. Loewen, Shawn (2004). *Second Language Concerns for Refugee Children.* In R. Hamilton & D. Moore (Eds.), *Educational Interventions for Refugee Children* (pp. 35–52). London: RoutledgeFalmer.

3. Tse, Lucy (2001). *Why Don't They Learn English? Separating Fact from Fallacy in the U.S. Language Debate.* New York Teachers College Press.

4. Loewen, Shawn (2004). *Second Language Concerns for Refugee Children.* In R. Hamilton & D. Moore (Eds.), *Educational Interventions for Refugee Children* (pp. 35–52). London: RoutledgeFalmer.

5. Bhattacharjee, Yudhijit (2012). *Why Bilinguals Are Smarter*, New York Times. Located at nyt.com. Retrieved June 2015.

6. Bhattacharjee, Yudhijit (2012). *Why Bilinguals Are Smarter*, New York Times. Located at nyt.com. Retrieved June 2015.

7. Examined Existence (2015). *12 Benefits of Learning A Foreign Language.* Examinedexistence.com. Retrieved July 2015.

8. Tse, Lucy (2001). *Why Don't They Learn English? Separating Fact from Fallacy in the U.S. Language Debate.* New York Teachers College Press.

9. Examined Existence (2015). *12 Benefits of Learning A Foreign Language.* Examinedexistence.com. Retrieved July 2015.

10. Loewen, Shawn (2004). *Second Language Concerns for Refugee Children.* In R. Hamilton & D. Moore (Eds.), *Educational Interventions for Refugee Children* (pp. 35–52). London: RoutledgeFalmer.

11. Dotson, Jeanie M. (2000). *Cooperative Learning Structures can Increase Student Achievement.* Fairmont, West Virginia.

12. Kagan, S. (1994). *Cooperative Learning.* San Clemente, California, Kagan Publishing.

13. Ridley, Lia (2003). *The Refugee Experience.* The Spring Institute, Denver.

14. Ridley, Lia (2003). *The Refugee Experience.* The Spring Institute, Denver.

15. Elliot, Doreen & Uma Segal (2012). *Refugees Worldwide, Vol 1: Global Perspectives.* Praeger Publishing.

16. Collet, Bruce. *Sites of Refuge: Refugees, Religiosity, and Public Schools in the United States.* Educational Policy. Vol. 24, No. 1, 189–215.

Chapter 7

Into Practice

Application and Implementation

ปฏิบัติที่ดีที่สุดในการเรียนการสอน –Thai

MAKING IT ALL COME TOGETHER: *A BRIEF INTRODUCTION TO THE CHAPTER*

So, *this* is why we're all here. Leaving all background and pedagogy aside, this is the part of the text that is most immediately applicable, meaningful, or digestible to us, as Newcomer educators. This is the meat; the part where we begin to put it all into practice.

Before we dive in, let's get one thing clear: I am not the expert here. *You* are.

I am an educator who happens to have a high level of experience working with refugee and Newcomer populations. This is what I am able to bring to the table, teacher to teacher. *You*, on the other hand, are the expert and authority in crafting quality education for your students. You know your learners' strengths and opportunities for continued growth; and you will be more capable of determining your students' needs than I could ever presume to be, as an outsider offering advice.

So, I'll just leave you with some potentially helpful items that I know, have learned, or have devised from trial and (sometimes explosive!) error. If the approaches that service our classroom also service yours, great! Hopefully, they can spur meaningful dialogue and continued professional development. In any case, take what you can and leave the rest.

Most importantly, pass along your own insights. Do not confine your secrets of the trade. After all, overarching educational success can only be realized if and when we are steadfast in holding our students as the heart of our craft. When we aim for the greatness of our learners, above the glory of ourselves and our practice, we all benefit. So share, grow, accept, and excel. Repeat.

In this chapter, we will begin to move away from history, fact, and precise pedagogy. From here, we will explore the ELA-E teaching practice at a very personal, approachable, and most importantly, applicable level. This is the part where we begin to define the craft for ourselves and seek out ways to better our craft together.

CREATING A FOUNDATION

Teaching in the Newcomer ELA-E realm of education is a whole different ball of wax. Really. When we step into a refugee and Newcomer classroom for the first time, so much of what we know about teaching goes right out the window. Modern Newcomer classrooms host a literal world of learners who are ultimately expected to excel alongside their mainstream peers. This is no small aim; and so the ELA-E landscape demands an entirely new brand of sheltered instruction.

Classroom Culture

What makes work and learning environments enjoyable? Common denominators include clarity, communication, and engagement. Performance is enhanced when expected outcomes are clear, protocol and procedure are in place, consistent meaningful feedback is available, and when participants are made to feel valued and important. When these items are in place, engagement and productivity flourish. Work and learning become *fun, impactful, and fulfilling.* These combined elements lay the groundwork for positive classroom culture.

In classroom and school settings, creating and maintaining a positive culture is essential. Achieving this aim requires patience, consistency, and determination. Below are key actions that enhance a positive school/classroom culture and climate.

Nurturing A Positive Learning Culture

Set high expectations, and make them explicit. Students, in most cases, will aim for the bar, wherever we set it. So mark it high.

1. Be organized. When we are prepared, little time is wasted. Also, students will imitate our behaviors. Let them mimic our very best qualities.

2. Communicate. Students should know what's happening, what has happened, and what is still to come. Be transparent. Involve parents in the knowing. Students and parents who feel informed are also likely to feel safe; safety leads to productivity.
3. Establish clear learning goals. Make them reasonable and attainable, but just beyond the rim of comfort. Review progress frequently and share growth results with students. Encourage learners to self-set goals for success and actively monitor progress.
4. Provide positive, constructive feedback. Students who do not receive feedback may be reinforcing the wrong things![1] This includes homework. The feedback piece is what makes it count. No cheating!
5. Establish healthy parameters. Most students desire structure. When students feel secure, they are liberated to learn.
6. Share the wheel. Students should have a say in what they are learning. Allow time for interest inventories and cooperative exchanges, which establish trust and spur ownership.
7. Keep things engaging. Learning should be fun!
8. Promote relationship building. Be committed to learning student names and correct pronunciations. Become a linguistic expert in hellos. Set embarrassment aside. We might sound ridiculous, but as we remind our students, it's the effort that counts. Encourage interaction, and be proactive in teaching and modeling positive behavior systems. Celebrate one another's achievements. Be an integral *part* of the classroom team.
9. Allow for choices and demonstrate trust in students' good decision making. Occasionally allow learners the opportunity to self-appoint station assignments. Cheer on responsible decision making, and address off-task students in ways that encourage self-evaluative behaviors. We want our learners to become efficient and self-guided, under the umbrella of structure and safety.
10. Embody positivity. Let students enjoy you as a positive person. Optimism, hope, and joy are contagious properties. We are teachers—what an opportunity to pass on the *best* character and learning qualities!

FINDING SQUARE ONE

Sitting in a Desk

Let's be clear: our precise field of choice is not for the lighthearted. We don't have many (or any) students who arrive with their own school supplies. Our parent volunteer lists are short or nonexistent. Many of our learners will enter school on the first snowy morning in some variation of a sandal. Some will need assistance in holding a pencil, and many will need assistance in navigating Western sanitation expectations. *Most* will be challenged to remain seated for any duration, leading up to the eight hours that they are in our care.

Here are a few suggestions:

Exercise Bands: Tied to the legs of a desk, children can kick at them without disturbing neighbors, but receiving kinesthetic stimuli.

Velcro Strips: These wonders are backed with adhesive, making them perfect for sticking just under the lip of a student's desk, just above where he or she would reach in for a pencil. Velcro strips or tabs come in a variety of textures. A soft piece and a structured piece together are a great combination. The student can rub the Velcro as they are engaging and participating.

Exercise Balls: Used as seats, exercise balls can stimulate and engage restless learners, and spur concentration, ultimately enhancing academic intake.

Fuzzy Balls/Feathers/Stress Balls: As long as students are reminded of the difference between tools and toys, these items can make focusing easier for individuals with tactile needs, without disrupting neighbors.

Pacing

Relative to native-speaking peers, Newcomers require increased intervals of time to process questions and responses in the host language. No big surprises here. Any of us who have attempted something new are likely to have experienced slow success at first; we pick up speed as we gain some familiarity with the task. With practice, we may become fluid and confident. So it goes with our young language learners.

Pacing is the element of allowing sufficient time for students to intake information in the host language, translate the concept into the native language, activate background knowledge when applicable, and formulate a host-language response. In the initial phases, this is rarely a three-second process. More like a very awkward, painful *53 seconds*.

Processing time is an accommodation. To enhance learners' input, an instructor should be clear and selective in his or her speech. It is also helpful when pacing is modified, such that the instructor maintains a slower rate of speech. Please note that an increased *volume* of speech is not considered supportive, and can very easily frustrate a child who has no problem hearing or thinking, but simply needs a few extra moments to digest input and output language content.

Effective pacing also makes room for extended response time. Often, students *know* the response they wish to produce, or have a clear understanding of a given concept in their minds. However, piecing words together in a new language requires separate faculties and new levels of concentration. With regard to cultural dynamics, children may also feel pressure to present only correct answers, including structure and agreement of speech, as a facet of the *saving face* piece. (See chapter 5)

Typically, *early host-language learners require between 30 and 45 seconds of uninterrupted time to process and respond to a question.*[2] This can be a challenge for us, as teachers, and also for other students. As native speakers of the West, we have a tendency—and sometimes expectation—for instantaneous results; and we are capable of demonstrating impatience in the interim. Ultimately, the teacher is expected to model endurance and vocal restraint during silent periods of anticipation.

Let the time pass patiently, without prompting. If, after an appropriate passage of time, the student is still struggling to produce a response, it may be wise to encourage the child in other ways. Ask the question in a new way that requires a less extensive response; have the child have a quick brainstorming session with his or her table-mates, and report back; or allow the learner to draw a picture of his or her idea on a Smart Board or other tool, and work as a class to label the illustration.

Routine

Routine and structure are critical in providing a sense of safety and security in a Newcomer classroom (or any classroom). Preestablished safety and security features can also support new students in acclimating to the new environment by providing comfort and allowing new students to pick up on social and contextual norms. Meanwhile, routine provides opportunities for learners to become *owners* of a task or concept, a precursor to self-efficacy. Thus, routine and structure promote academic and social gain in a multitude of ways.

Routines are actions that are initially explicitly taught, but which learners can ultimately complete with limited or no guided assistance. Established procedures aid students in making sense of the new environment through predictability, while providing clarity with regard to participation and behavior expectations.[3] As a result, classroom routines allow for increased teacher instructional time and enhanced student-learning opportunities.[4]

The best time to teach any routine is always *at the beginning*. Routine and structure must be modeled and practiced relentlessly in the initial phases. Lasting success is contingent upon ongoing implementation and constructive teacher feedback. In fact, routine is the cornerstone in producing and maintaining any classroom learning or behavior routine.

Gestures

Universal signs and body language can play a critical role in the initial stages of understanding and language acquisition. These important visual and social cues act as critical frames of reference for the ELA learner. They serve as anchors of primary comprehension, from which thorough language learning can take root.

Gesturing and body language add depth of understanding that is not exclusive to language learning. We've all experienced it: hands on the hips, tapping fingers, a smile, a wink, a wave, a yawn. We can make sense of these gestures without the need for a translator.

We act out gestures in the classroom, too. In fact, as teachers, we have a reputation for it. We are masters of the *shhh* pointer finger to the lips, the *stop* hand sign, and the *Give Me Five*. Educators are champions of gesturing.

In the Newcomer classroom, gestures are physical, and enunciated. In a Level One classroom, instructions to *sit down* could be accompanied by the motion of sitting down in an invisible chair. *Open your book* may be accentuated with hand gestures that imply the same. *Write* can be demonstrated by engraving into the air. Charades, anyone? It sounds like too much—but it can, and does, help!

Before getting too carried away, there are a few parameters worth noting. First, gestures should only be used when essential or meaningful. As the student progresses in his or her language understanding, it is reasonable to move away from incorporating cues into every facet of communication. Signals should not become a crutch; and new language learners also need to enjoy examples of normal, fluid body language in the new setting. Second, it is important to be cognizant of specific gestures that may be the norm in the host setting, but which might be considered rude or offensive in a Newcomer's home culture. (See chapter 5)

That's it. Get gesturing. Make it big, pronounced, subtle, small, serious, or silly. Be bold in encouraging students to join in. Make it fun and comprehensible. These are elements of creative learning!

Realia and Visuals

Newcomer learning is greatly supported and enhanced through the use of visuals and three-dimensional stimuli. As they say, a picture is worth a thousand words. In that case, something to hold in your hand is worth a million.

Realia and visuals are conduits between content knowledge and student experience. They are tangible strands of connectivity, and they carry the potential to engage students across all sensory platforms. With specific regard to ELL learning, "using concrete objects in the classroom creates cognitive connections with vocabulary, stimulates conversation, and builds background knowledge; [and it] gives students the opportunity to use all of their senses to learn about a subject."[5]

The term *realia* refers to physical objects that can be touched, seen, smelled, heard, or tasted, thus engaging one or more of the human senses. When concrete items cannot be made available, alternative sensory cues can be employed, such as artwork, illustrations, photographs, or demonstrations. A caution: "Each move down the continuum [of concrete realia] causes the loss of some sensory information that could be helpful in comprehension."[6]

Realia can be easily incorporated into daily practice. Make a fruit salad to learn fruit names. Take a nature walk to learn about trees or environment. Bring in the horseshoe, the suspenders, the toothpick, the frying pan, the bank deposit slips, the vinyl record, the rake, and the scarecrow. Then, let students *talk* about it.

Visuals and realia can engage and motivate students. Beyond this, concrete evidence in the classroom can make understanding more digestible, impactful, and permanent. This is one means of connecting language to life, and having fun doing it!

Examples:

- Utilization of international currency as counting manipulatives, play money, class incentive, or as the basis for social studies projects.
- Post cards, stamps, maps, tourism brochures as a launch point for geography study.
- Animal fur, horseshoes, photos, collars, leashes, sound clips, feathers, leaves, pinecones, or sand for natural study.
- Bowties, shoe laces, buttons, zippers, mittens, denim, jewelry, sunglasses for clothing identification and literary character study.
- Sandpaper, velvet, cotton balls, wax candles, pennies, pipe cleaners for texture/adjective study.

ACTIVATING BACKGROUND KNOWLEDGE

"What can this new word, *weaving,* mean?" I asked our third-grade Newcomer class. I was referring to text in a book about Native American rabbits. "I don't know, Ms. K., but I think that's the thing that my grandmother know how to do for a long time, like this." Kankou, from Mali, demonstrated with her hands. "She try to teach me, but I always forgot how it goes."

The conversation continued. Saw Min Oo from Burma announced, "Oh, yeah, Ms. K. And do you know, the womens in my country they put those things that you we-weav . . . how do you say it? They put those things on their heads to carry everything to eat." This remark set the entire rest of the class off. *Oh, yes. They do that in my country, too. And they put the rice in there*

*for the market. And we have big, big things that go on the floor for everybody
to sleep on. It looks like the same. That is weaving also, Ms. K.?*

Activating background knowledge is a critical component of the learning process. It is of particular value in guiding Newcomer learners through
the combined language learning and literacy processes. By activating background knowledge, learners have access to added layers of depth and comprehension. For Newcomers, activation of prior knowledge and experience
promotes opportunities to acquire essential vocabulary in meaningful ways.

Background knowledge holds a prized place in the Newcomer classroom.
We remind students: use what you know. There are so many different kinds
of knowledge; and not all of it comes from a classroom. You can use *your life*
to help you read a book. And they do. When the words come, they also love
to share their background connections. In this space, recollections of pertinent
life experiences are activated, and comprehension is expedited.

MODELING

Modeling, or teaching through demonstrated behaviors, is the way we've
been taught to teach in every class, seminar, and handbook. It's also among
the most influential ways in which we've accumulated our own unique talent
and skill sets. Usually, modeling is coupled with instructional scaffolds. In
classroom talk, we refer to this as "I Do, We Do, You Do."

In this scenario, the mentee(s) will first observe the mentor as he or she
physically and/or verbally walks through a specific task or procedure. Next,
the mentor and mentee(s) will complete the activity process together, with the
teacher available to guide, correct, and encourage the learner along the way.
Finally, the mentee will attempt the task alone, with limited or no assistance.

This is the way of turning over ownership of an aim or task. There is a
reason we hear so much about teaching through modeling and instructional
scaffolds. These are effective processes that produce positive end results.
In fact, modeling has proven itself a valuable means of relaying information
and skills for perhaps the entirety of human existence, ranking it among the
oldest and most effective instructional tools. Why *wouldn't* we employ the
practice in our classrooms?

MANIPULATIVES

Manipulatives are fun and engaging; and satisfy specific needs for visual and
kinesthetic learners. They are hands-on tools that really *do* accentuate student
growth and understanding.

So, let's get right to the point. Get them out of the closet. Keep them organized and make them accessible. Incorporate manipulatives in as many applicable and purposeful means as possible. Often, early language learners can *show* what they know, even when telling or explaining is a challenge. Let them demonstrate. Then, let them practice some more, adding new pieces of content vocabulary. Eventually, learners will be able to explain their thoughts at any varying level of capacity.

Often, the school will provide some basic manipulative sets, especially for math. Not so? Try these! Here's a short list of dollar store finds that are fun and functional in the classroom.

MANIPULATIVES SUGGESTIONS

• Dice: counting, probability, number bump, place value, counting, reading response, bingo
• Fuzzy balls/Cotton Balls: counting, soundless tactile-need quantifier
• Floss: measuring tape, length, and perimeter
• Rubber Bands; around a cup: counting, tens, fine motor skills
• Pebbles: sorting, counting, weight, painted-on dominos
• Feathers: sorting, weight, soundless tactile-need quantifier (sped)
• Buttons: sorting (with egg tray or muffin tin), counting, measurement, tracing letters
• Cheeze-Its: area and perimeter, shapes, counting
• Counting Bears: sorting, counting, measurement
• Wax candles, bobby pins, sandpaper, straws, pennies, felt: adjective study, counters
• Post-It Notes: fraction strips, patterns, writing, editing
• Marshmallows: volume, counting, graphing, sorting, shapes
• Bottle/Jug lids: capital-lower case, math facts or other match (write on lid)
• Leggos ®- Base ten: sorting, patterns, place value
• Gummy worms/M&Ms/Skittles: measurement, graphing, sorting, counting
• Paper plates: clocks, fraction pies, counting cards, lacing trays
• Popsicle sticks: base ten, bundling, number line, sentence strips, perimeter
• Cardboard: lacing boards, tangrams, geoboard
• Toothpicks: base ten, bundling, three-dimensional shape (with marshmallows)
• Beans and Seeds: counting, sorting, graphing
• Index cards: sentence strips, word chunking blocks, memory
• Measuring Cups: measurement concepts, play
• Pool Noodles: base ten, area, perimeter, measurement
• Plastic Spoons: letter/number match, time

- Marbles: sorting, counting, fine motor activities (with tweezers)
- Shoe Laces: lacing cards, bead counting, measurement, area/perimeter
- Paper clips/clothespins: color matching, counting, sorting, spelling, compound words
- Sponges: stamping, sorting, stacking

TECHNOLOGY

Technology skills are pertinent assets for all of our learners as they embark upon life beyond the learning institution. Technology skills in relation to twenty-first-century success are no longer a commodity. They are a necessity. In the Newcomer setting, access to modern resources in the home may be especially limited. Thus, we have an extra duty to provide our students with rich opportunities to practice and grow in their technological skills and awareness.

We can promote classroom technology exposure and use in a variety of ways. Computers are usually the first example of technology to come to mind, and rightfully so. Computers are a vital component in almost every part of the school day. Attendance and email, iPods and iPads, online planners, and Smart Board interaction—computer intelligence is intertwined with most aspects of classroom functioning. We might have any varying level of access to these resources within our schools and districts.

In any case, it is important to work effectively and efficiently with what we do have. We can begin by knowing the equipment. Technology doesn't mean a thing if it cannot be properly or effectively operated. Take a class to improve your own skills, if necessary. Be open to trying and learning new things, and become dedicated to employing technological resources in the classroom.

The bottom line is that our learners require technology skill sets in order to be successful in almost any future work capacity. In this and coming generations, computer, engineering, science, and math facilities are an absolute value, if not an outright requirement for workplace security. In short, technological exposure and experience is an invaluable asset for our students, as they prepare to meet future real-world demands.

For a kick start, visit the ELL technology resources pages and lesson ideas in chapter 9, Twenty-First-Century Learning.

GRAPHIC ORGANIZERS

Graphic organizers are a means of making concepts tangible, digestible, and engaging! For second language learners, graphic organizers satisfy the visual stimulation piece that can be so critical to vocabulary development. Essentially, graphic organizers allow students to meaningfully participate in content learning at a variety of linguistic skill and academic ability levels.

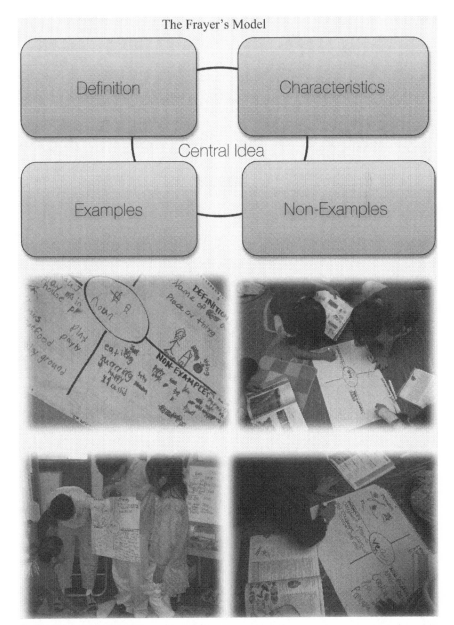

Figure 7.2 Frayer model

The gamut of organizers is extensive. In fact, it is very likely that we already employ at least some of them to enhance learning in our classrooms. Here, we'll highlight a few favorites. Put them to use when and where they are applicable to you and your learners.

The Frayer Model

The Frayer model is a well-known resource that was created by educator Dorothy Frayer as an avenue for bringing depth and personal meaning to generic word study.[7] It is a terrific tool for individual work, station work, unit anchor charts, formative assessments, and summative assessments. In the center of the diagram, learners record the main idea or focus topic. The remaining quadrants are reserved for: definition (upper right), illustrations (upper left), examples (lower right), and non-examples (lower left). Participants can utilize any and all available resources to assist them.

Frayer model charts can be completed as a solitary activity. However, in the Newcomer setting, they prove especially beneficial as carefully orchestrated cooperative activities. Generally, it is best to assign groups of two or four. Ideally, students are matched at a high-to-low ability levels. In other words, each group should have a high and a low performer, or a high/low/mid/mid-proficiency ratio.

Preliminary language learners make excellent candidates for the *illustrations* bloc, and have the aim of labeling all or most of the nouns represented in the drawing. Higher functioning participants work well in the definition and examples categories. Mid-ability learners are likely to succeed (or be encouraged toward a deeper level of rigor) in any quadrant.

Butcher paper or large post-it paper works well for group Frayer charts. Depending on teacher preference, students may be invited to sprawl out with their respective groups as needed. Picture match dictionaries, student journals, unit vocabulary/picture cards, and any other tools should be readily accessible to learners. In addition, students' academic interchange (using posted collaborative sentence stems) should be highly encouraged; conversation is celebrated!

Frayer charts work especially well as reading group and science learning activities, and can also function as genre *reports*. In this way, separate small sets of students will record information about different topics using the Frayer model (food groups, animal families, relatives, space objects, etc.). Ultimately, groups present completed work to a peer audience.

Student teams typically *love* having the floor to share their finished pieces. This portion of a Frayer-based lesson addresses the oral speaking element. This is a wonderful time to practice oral fluency and complete sentence speaking (with sentence stem starters as necessary) and boost oral production through team member support.

Venn Diagrams

Venn diagrams are a classic means of comparing and contrasting two elements of learning. Venn charts are comprised of two (or three) overlapping circles, each individual circle labeled with a specific item of study. The external portions of each circle are reserved for naming properties or qualities unique to the respective topic. The central portion of the diagram speaks to characteristics that are shared between the two.

Venn diagrams are terrific instruments for expressions, especially for limited English proficient (LEP) students. These tools allow learners to demonstrate concept understanding, minus the demand for complete sentence production. At the earliest stages of language acquisition, Venn diagrams can incorporate pictures, leading to labeled pictures, and graduating to language-rich compositions. Venn charts can also function as a cooperative learning structure, when pairs or small groups of students are encouraged to complete and verbally present their work as a team.

There are no limits to comparative possibility. Venn diagrams are cross-curricular formative assessment tools capable of providing valid snapshots of comprehension and understanding. Other student-friendly graphic organizers include:

- *Vocabulary Concentration:* Frayer Model, Word Map, Describing Wheel, Story Map, Fish Map, Spider Map
- *Reading & Comprehension:* Story Panel, Story Elements Chart, Character/Trait Profile, Character Analysis, K-W-L, Student Response Log, Fact/Opinion Chart
- *Main Idea & Detail:* Fish Map—5Ws + How; Sun Map; Cause-Effect Flow Chart
- *Compare & Contrast:* Venn Diagram
- *Writing Organizers:* Hamburger Writing Template, Stoplight Organizer, Planning Flow Charts; Rubrics and Writing checklists; Outlines; Book Report Templates

SYMBOLS AND SYMBOLISM

Symbolism is evidenced in nearly every aspect of the human experience. Symbols are intrinsically imbedded mechanisms of social interchange that facilitate and enhance interpersonal communication. Symbolic code structures exist among family members, tribes and clans, and geographic and religious cultures; and they thrive within our own classrooms.

Most symbolic structures are shared, either by direct transference, or indirectly, as a byproduct of environment, exposure, and experience. Certain symbols are unique to a particular set of peoples. Symbol-rich arenas include language, dance, art, song, literature, ritual, value structures, and goal setting.

American culture takes pride in its own symbols: the U.S. flag, the bald eagle, the White House, or the Liberty Bell. It is necessary (and often very exciting) for our Newcomer students to become familiar with American imagery and symbolism. Now, what if we paused to invite classroom conversation and exploration regarding the symbols of other nations and cultures?

International students often connect intensely with home-culture symbolism, and they may be energized to share these details in a safe setting. These occasions make for extraordinary teaching moments. Meanwhile, encouraging students to take ownership of their thoughts and words in positive and meaningful ways fosters a healthy, engaging, and tolerant classroom culture.

Outside of religious symbolism, flags are one of the most globally recognized symbols of geographical belongingness and group identity. Invite students to consider the composition of the U.S. flag: *Why red, white, and blue? What is the meaning of the stars? The stripes?* Next, encourage students to draw (or research and draw) the flag of their native country and to express what they already know about the nature and meaning of their flag. Learners can share their work through cooperative structures. A class endeavor may be to highlight a culture each month or week, expanding on other meaningful symbols.

TIME

Time can be an elusive concept for young people as a whole. In working with Newcomer ELLs, it is additionally helpful to note that each culture honors the passage of time in a unique way. In urban America, for example, time is a precious commodity. It is treasured, hoarded, and calculated to the minute. Ours is a culture enrapt with appointments, bells, and deadlines. If there is one thing we Americans know, it is time.

Pa Leh Paw's concept of time holds different value. Just before her eighth birthday, Pa Leh Paw's father explained to her that they would have to leave behind their beloved home in an affluent district of Burma. She left with her family in the blackness of the night, with her younger brother and a rolled-up sleeping mat on her back; she did not cry at all. Pa Leh's family made up one-third of a traveling band.

Together, the posse endured two months and 200 miles of traversing jungle and waterways before reaching the haven of their Thailand refugee camp.

From their look-out house on stilts, time was evident: it was day when the sun came up and evening when the dense foliage swallowed up the sun. Months surfaced and disappeared at the whim of the moon. Time was present, but also a presence, elongated and meaningful.

And so now, you want to teach Pa Leh Paw *third-grade* time, on a manipulative *Judy* clock. You want her to perform well on the state exams. You want her to be successful in the world outside of your classroom. You want to prove that you are doing your job, teaching her about time. And it seems that there will never be enough time to do it!

In many cultures and countries, time and scheduling are not highly regarded as they are in the West. In most of the developing world (and also in some developed nations), interpersonal connections maintain precedence over the value of time. As a result, time and schedule adherence may not be honored or demanded, at least as it is in the westernized sense.

Accordingly, many of our students may not have been exposed to the same level of schedule structuring and time management tactics that we, in the West, have been accustomed to our entire lives. Thus, classroom routine and consistency play an especially important role in promoting an awareness of time and time increments. As students begin to understand the concept of *lunch at 11:30; specials at 2:30; and bell at 3:45,* time (and the expectations that are associated with it) becomes relevant. Relevance breeds learning.

Creating classroom clocks can be a helpful exercise in making time relevant and manipulative. Students are involved, engaged, interacting, identifying, naming, and problem solving. The process can also be fun; and it allows the learners a take-home or station tool that can be used again and again.

There are lots of options for making this activity come to life. Paper plates and brad clips are one simple, on-hand version. Whole class kinesthetic versions also work well. DIY clocks present fantastic opportunities to practice critical baseline skills: hours and minutes; elapsed time; counting by 5s; counting by 10s; rounding/estimation; and fractions.

SHELTERED INSTRUCTION AND APPLICATION CONCEPTS FOR ELLs

English language learners do not require a lower grade of academics, or less rigorous curricula. They do, however, necessitate alternative avenues for accessing and transmitting critical information. It is professional responsibility/educator's responsibility to pave these routes and to direct our learners toward them. Here, we'll investigate a few potential paths to follow.

Game Time!

Games, by their very nature, encourage critical thinking, healthy communication, and teamwork. Moreover, they are *designed* to be fun! Intellectual playtime can also serve a purposeful role in classroom education.

Game-structure activities, when intentionally planned and strategically implemented, can have tremendous effects on learning. First, game play encourages healthy participation, which means that students are self-motivated, self-evaluating, and intrinsically invested. It also enhances communication skills, considering that unknown knowledge, rules, and variables must be transposed from one student to another, especially when a whole team effort is required.

Positive game play also services students who are less willing to be risk takers in the strict academic sense, as part of the cultural *saving face* mechanism. Learning in a game context may lessen student pressure to attempt only *right* answers, as mistakes or errors in play may not be perceived as critical missteps. Students are also likely to support and encourage one another's attempts, valid or not, when a learning activity is perceived as a puzzle or game. As a result, educationally relevant game play also lends itself to community building, trust opportunities, and positive social interchange.

Hopscotch and jump rope are examples of games that promote learning. These games are considered international pastimes. Most Newcomer students will have some previous exposure to hopscotch and jump rope activities, and most connections are positive ones.

These types of kinesthetic games can be employed to practice word sounds and spelling, among other things. Students call out specified letters, sounds, or syllables as they hop. Correct replies indicate a *move* to the next level; inaccurate responses result in another round or retry. This can be done individually, or in small teams. In the small group scenario, a "numbered heads" approach works well. After team members brainstorm together, one teammate shares out the group response.

Both games can be used to practice, in addition to word sounds and spelling, any of the following and more: the alphabet, names, months, days of the week, vowels, spelling, counting and skip counting, math facts, scientific stages, and story sequencing. This can also be a fun time to learn and incorporate jump rope, hopscotch, or handclapping rhymes from students' cultures! Games can be played outside or inside on a masking tape floor template.

It may also be helpful to provide a World Games station. Allow students to share activities from their home countries, or seek out others, such as Mancala (Asia and Africa), GO (East Asia), or Ludo (India). These types of games encourage strategy and problem-solving skills.

Textile Manipulation

Textiles, especially those unique to our students' home countries, make excellent learning foundations and extensions. Waxed fabric prints and other textile mediums are extremely popular in most developing nations, and are a particular highlight of the African continent. Employed as a means of fostering academic understanding, critical thinking, and artistic creativity, print patterns and textiles can be an integral and impactful part of classroom engagement.

Wearable textiles include African kanga print cloths, East Indian and Nepalese patterned saris, and traditional Burmese and Thai longyi designs. Similarly, beadwork arrays, weaving, quilting, cross-stitch, tile laying, crochet patterns, and mural decorations qualify as textile art; and each medium can offer up a gold mine of valuable teaching opportunities.

As a form of tangible realia, textiles can generate opportunities for connection, communication, and enriched understanding. It is additionally beneficial to incorporate multicultural examples of textiles as an endorsement for healthy sharing of students' cultures and customs. In this way, the process can provide for general global awareness and serve as a conduit for promoting cross-cultural tolerance.

All this, and we have not even begun talking about the academic utility of textile use in the classroom! Textile prints and patterns can be applied to engage students in a variety of learning objectives. For example, students can use textiles to explore the nature of geometric shapes, lines, and patterns, algebraic sense making, topology, graphing theory, number theory, color identification, and community/national color significance, among other topics.

Students also enjoy manufacturing their own textile pieces. This form of kinesthetic participation encourages creative design, pattern recognition, abstract reasoning, and problem-solving skill sets to flourish. The good news for teachers is that textile production in the classroom *can* take place within limited time, workspace, and budget constraints. Bead work patterns are only one example of this. Alternative classroom-friendly "textile" mediums and supplies include the following:

Table 7.1 Textile Manipulation

Noodles	Cotton balls	Yarn
Candy	Cereal	Pipe-cleaners
Toothpicks	Quilt squares	Pom-poms
Buttons	Natural outdoor fibers	Popcorn
Sea shells	Food coloring designs	Paper bags & paint
Tissue paper squares	White t-shirts and markers	Cupcake sprinkles

Dramatic Play and Physical Expression of Thought

Dramatic play is a natural and inherent piece of healthy child development, fostering both language and intellectual capabilities. Dramatics are pertinent to the Newcomer classroom in that they allow for expressed emotion and understanding, even with limited use of the host language. Learners who have not yet become comfortable in the new language framework have an opportunity to discover a "voice" through acting-out processes. These types of constructive experiences can be freeing for the student, revealing for the educator, and base building for the learning community. Beyond all of this, drama is just plain, old-fashioned fun!

One outcome of dramatic play is emotional exploration. Emotional exploration that occurs within a sheltered environment can provide many benefits, especially working with resettled refugee populations, where grief and traumatic exposure are routinely elevated. In positive, carefully crafted settings, dramatic learning structures can provide safe and healthy platforms for combined emotional and vocabulary growth. Meanwhile, theatrics function as a valid comprehension assessment that can be exclusive of the language piece.

For example, guided role-play, in which students silently act out various emotions, can satisfy the aim of associating specific facial features and body language with a given circumstance. In a literary setting, learners may be asked to show a character's facial expressions (link: feelings); or to mime or act out character traits, actions, or whole scenes. As it is said, *the best way to know something is to be it.* Here are a few fun starters![8,9]

1. Create A Human Machine

   Begin with one or two connected children creating a simple, repetitive sound. Children contribute to the *machine* by entering the work space one at a time, connecting to another part of the machine by some body part, and adding a new beep, honk, bend, squat, jump, or squish. After: Discuss questions, insights, new vocabulary, and celebrated demonstrations of creativity.

2. "Two Noses"

   Invite students to circumambulate the room. Facilitator calls out a) a number and b) a body part. Learners respond to the prompt by aligning themselves with the appropriate number of people, touching at the corresponding body part. For example, three elbows would play out with three students connected to each other in some way by their elbows. Encourage children to be creative in their connective choices and formations. This process continues: 4 knees, 6 thumbs, 2 backs, or 5 shins. This is a fun and creative means of team building; it also functions as a valuable opportunity for vocabulary acquisition.

3. Still Pictures/Tableaus

Working in small groups, students create frozen *snapshots* of a scene from a text. Tableaus can capture setting, character thought or emotion, and sequence of events. This is terrific for group work, and also as a means of evaluating individual understanding and participation.

4. Act It Out

Read and discuss a text with students (*The Hungry Caterpillar*, for example), and then ask them play out the story alongside a narration. This is an entertaining process for all involved! More than this, dramatic role-play is engaging and meaningful for the students, and it meanwhile offers educators a valid formative assessment of learner comprehension. Other ideas: plant life cycle, character reaction, imaginative journey (to another planet, say), migration trails, bullying responses, historical enactments, or the *life* of a drop of water. This is also a great activity for acting out dialogue or the sequence of events in a story or text.

5. True Theatrics

Simple plays at early reading levels are fantastic for developing and practicing reading fluency. Mask making can incorporate a host of various cultural and country traditions. Puppetry allows for student creativity, reading fluency, imaginative skills, and the ability to *act* without fully revealing or exposing themselves. Set the stage!

6. Human Knot

Students form a close circle, hands open and facing toward the center of the circle. Each participant reaches for two hands. The hands should not belong to the same person, or be joined to an immediate neighbor. *Slowly,* and with some coaching, students try to unravel their human knot without disconnecting their hands. This process stimulates teamwork, problem-solving skills, and creativity.

7. Treasure Chest

Students sit in a circle. One student is blindfolded and stands inside the circle. An object (scarf, piece of paper, stuffed animal) is placed somewhere inside the circle. Taking turns, participants will guide the blindfolded learner to the *treasure chest*, practicing the usage of descriptive and clear directions. (*Take three baby steps forward, then turn right. . .*) Exchange roles. This process enables students to give and follow prompts, practice directional cue words, and creatively problem solve toward a solution.

8. One Word Story

Sitting in a circle, the first person offers a single word to begin a story. The next person contributes the second word of the story, and so on. The story may shift and change unexpectedly, but should ultimately find closing. This exercise is great for sense making, sequencing, and vocabulary building; meanwhile, it is a fun team-building activity. Certain parameters may be set in advance (theme, topic, unit vocabulary). Recorded sessions are excellent opportunities for practicing recorded dictation and/or recall, story continuation, and listening station options, among others.

9. What Are You Doing?

Divide students in half; one group will be an audience. The acting group of students forms two straight lines vertically facing the audience. One of the two students in front begins a verb motion (for example, eating lunch). The other student asks, *What Are You Doing?* The first student replies with a new verb. *I'm brushing my teeth.*

The second student immediately begins acting out this verb, while the first student goes to the back of his or her line. The next student in line steps up and asks, *"What are you doing?"* The active student responds with a new verb, *I'm driving my car*, and returns to the back of the line. The process continues until all players have had a turn. Actors and audience reverse.

This is a fantastic vocabulary-building game! For ELLs—if a student can create an action, but is without the English word for it, the audience may kindly assist! A *high five* to the audience can signal, "Help me out, here!" *Both* sides love this!

10. Miming

Give a specific direction. Model miming exact directive. For example, *Sharpen your pencil. Open your book. Think. Have an idea. Feel the window and look out.* Invite students to join. Continue, without modeling. This is a great exercise to check for understanding without language restriction. Miming is also effective for story lines and plot directives.

11. Mock Interviews

Author study? Character study? New science material? Covering world topics or key figures in history? Perfect for an interview! Students can conduct this activity in pairs, or as a larger group interviewing a *panel of experts.* Many learners, especially ELLs, may need specific insight and modeling regarding the interviewer/interviewee relationship. Graphic organizers specific to the topic may also be very useful for recording responses.

12. Scene Improvisations

Students divide into small teams. Each team selects an index card with a scenario or location (*at the grocery store; on the bus; at the pool; at a birthday party; at the zoo; learning to ride a bike; losing a tooth*). Teams act out the scenario or a short bit that would reveal the location, without actually saying the actual name of the scenario/locale aloud. Observing teams will attempt to guess the index card cue correctly.

13. Emotion Party

Have students pretend that they are going to a fancy party. One student, acting as the host, will begin in the *stage space* alone, waiting for guests to arrive. Another student will *knock* on the door, and be let in by the host. The guest, without using words, will show an emotion. (Silent emotions may work best in the classroom setting). The host, upon understanding the new emotion, will immediately assume the same energy.

A new guest will arrive, with a new emotion. Everyone at the party will demonstrate this new emotion, and so on, until all guests have arrived. Once everyone has had a turn to enter, each will leave in the order they arrived, with the emotion they came with.

This is a wonderful chance to explore emotions. Beginning learners will demonstrate simple facial expressions, and will match them with baseline vocabulary—happy, sad, mad, or tired. More advanced students will be able to apply other body language and may also be able to reach beyond basic word use, exploring higher level synonyms and altogether new ranges of emotion. For emotion examples, see Word Strength, Chapter 6.

FOOD FOR THOUGHT

The sharing of food, in most countries and cultures around the world, is synonymous with family, community, hospitality, respect, giving, heritage, and history. In a Newcomer classroom, food sharing can manifest itself into building blocks for verbal exchange, cross-cultural appreciation, and affirmation of one's heritage value. A few project ideas:

• Use traditional nonperishable foods, for example, Betel Nuts (used in Nepal, Bhutan, India, Burma, Thailand, etc.) as counters and manipulatives.
• Create a class or school version of an international cookbook. Or, invite students to prepare and present oral reports about important foods from their home countries.
• Discuss fruits and vegetables found in other countries and continents. Name vegetables in alternative classroom languages. Create a class alphabet based on fruits found in students' countries. Enjoy a shared multicultural classroom feast.
• Explore international spices as an adjective study. Soak cotton balls in various scents and have students (blindfolded or not) use English words to describe, and ultimately name, the scents that they smell.
• Engage students in researching/sharing/identifying/renaming country and culture-relevant spices and flavorings. Curry, clove, cinnamon, cardamom,

parsley, betel nut, green pepper, ginger, garlic, pine nut, pomegranate, chili, lemon, 7 Spices, zatar, sumac, sesame, basil, oregano, and cilantro are interesting options.

- Incorporate cultural food boxes and cans in interactive play (class *shopping* or *kitchen* centers).
- Hold *Ask Me Anything* sessions regarding American food. (Many Newcomers are not accustomed to cheese, fast food, or high sugar snacks; and pork or beef may be off-limits foods. A typical lunch, school pepperoni cheese pizza, packs a double whammy!)
- To this end, invite students to become proactive in initiating school meal reform . . . while targeting persuasive writing.
- Enlist students to conduct nutritional surveys of typical meals in their home countries. What are the nutritional advantages? Deficits? For further reference, compare to diet trends in the new country. Keep going with an analysis of anticipated daily physical exertion in the two countries. What lifestyle choices might the student determine are in his/her best interest and why?

OUTDOOR EXPLORATION

Outdoor learning engages sensory and kinesthetic learners and makes understanding approachable. Open-space exploration can also encourage problem-solving skills and relieve anxiety and stress. Meanwhile, this use of time provides terrific opportunities for host-culture students to experience the new surroundings and discover new language in participatory ways.

A few thoughts: nature walks; field trips; plant and animal study; scavenger hunts; shape finds; science note booking; gardening (area, perimeter, measurement, design, responsibility); community service and shadow learning; interviews; workplace visits; and arts exploration.

MUSICAL EXTENSIONS

Most children love to sing songs. Also, melody is a tried-and-true means for making learning concrete. Research demonstrates that musical exposure strengthens brain connections, and promotes appropriate cognitive and emotional development. Lyrics set to music may also increase memory and introduce listeners to new vocabulary, thus enhancing literacy skill sets.

When movement is also incorporated (through dance, action, or instrument playing), kinesthetic pathways are also activated. See the lyrics to one traditional camp classic, "Apples and Bananas," for a perfect way to learn the long vowels!

Most Newcomer curricula designs now incorporate songs. Seek out new ones to suit specific learning topics (GoNoodle is a great place to start). Or, invent your own, as a teacher or as a whole class. Students of all ages shine when songs are involved!

EVERY MOMENT COUNTS

Effective ELL/ELA-E classrooms share in certain key values. They are grounded in sheltered instruction techniques and best-practice applications; and they foster positive classroom culture. Yet, no two Newcomer classrooms are the same. Each looks, sounds, and feels differently. In short, there is no one "right" way. There are thousands of them.

When we go out of our way to make learning an enjoyable and interactive process for our students, we help to create lifelong learners. Also, when we feel engaged, our students are more likely to be engaged. Engagement lends itself to productivity, and productivity to success. As a result, we help our students grow; and we also define our own *work* as more fulfilling, gratifying, and purposeful.

So how do we do that *now?* How can we expand upon it even further? How can we enhance our potential effectiveness as educators and maximize our students' capacity for high achievement?

There are no absolute answers to these questions anywhere in this text (or in any other). We are all in search of our own *right* answers, for ourselves and for our practice. Interestingly, one teacher's *perfect fit* would drive another educator crazy; and that educator's mode of effective instruction, to some others, would seem bananas. That's the whole point.

This is our art. Picasso and Degas are incredibly dissimilar masterminds of their craft; yet both are brilliantly awe-inspiring. So it goes with our teaching (and also our students' learning). There are no one-size-fits-all programs. As for these and any insights shared with us in the field, alter, adjust, skip, test, and employ. As long as we are in the process of trying, we are also in the process of growing and sharing. In the end, that is precisely what our entire field is all about.

NOTES

1. Kazin, Brenda. Principal, Place Bridge Academy, Refugee Magnate school in Denver, Colorado. Interview, August 17, 2015.
2. Hakuta, K. ButlHakuta, K., Butler, Y. G., & Witt, D. (2000). *How Long does it Take English Learners to Attain Proficiency?* Located at from: http://lmri.ucsb.edu/publications/00_hakuta.pdf. Retrieved March 2010.

3. Burden, P. & D. Byrd (2003). *Methods for Effective Teaching: Meeting the Needs of All Students* (5th Edition) Pearson Education.

4. Kaser, Catherine Hoffman, M.A., (2014). *Classroom Environment.* Old Dominion University. Located at https://www.odu.edu/content/dam/odu/col-dept/cdse/docs/1-classroom-environments.pdf. Retrieved March 2015.

5. Arizona Department of Education (2011). *English Language Learner Guide for Local Educational Agencies.* Located at azed.gov. Retrieved Oct. 2012.

6. Herrell, Adrienne L. & Michael L. Jordan (2012). *Fifty Strategies for Teaching English Language Learners* (4th Edition). Pearson Publishing.

7. Blachowicz, C., Fisher, P., Ogle, D. & Watts-Taffe, S. (2013). *Teaching Academic Vocabulary K-8: Effective Practices across the Curriculum.* New York: Guilford Press.

8. Piaget, J. (1962). *Play, Dreams and Imitation in Childhood.* New York.

9. Stewig and Buege (1994). *Dramatizing Literature in Whole Language Classrooms.* New York: Teachers College Press.

Chapter 8

ELA-E Literacy Foundations

Reading Platforms and Multicultural Text

ਪੜ੍ਹਨ ਬੁਨਿਆਦ, ਅਤੇ ਬਹੁ ਸਾਹਿਤ - Punjabi

SUPPORTING THE NEWCOMER AS AN EMERGENT READER ACROSS THE ELD SPECTRUM

English is a complex language, hallmarked by intricacy, variant meaning, and rules just made to be broken. With its dialects, slang, idioms, and remarkable fetish for homonymic words, the depth of the English language is cavernous. It is an enormous undertaking for any budding reader.

Several separate rubrics are used to identify reading readiness and mark learners' progress in the arena of language acquisition. These can include the Five Stages of Language Acquisition; Basic Interpersonal Communication Skills (BICS); Cognitive Academic Language Proficiency (CALP); and WIDA Can-Do benchmarks (World-class Instructional Design and Assessment). Single language acquisition rubrics are rarely used in isolation. Rather, they are employed in conjunction with other indicators, including the standard stages of Reading Development (and others not referenced above).

Here, we'll look into the dominant rubrics.

Five Stages of Language Acquisition

The Stages of Language Acquisition Development is a gradient schedule for speaking, listening, and writing abilities in the new language. The continuum follows five stages: pre-production, early production, speech emergence, intermediate language fluency, and continuant language development.

Each category may be further subdivided for increased specificity. Below is a brief analysis of the overarching branches.[1]

Pre-Production

In this forefront stage of language acquisition, learners are just beginning to explore essential elements of the new language. This period is often aligned with initial host language exposure. It is a time of listening, absorbing, sense making, and gesturing.

Sense making is the most critical function of the pre-production stage, and most cognitive energies will be directed toward this end. Oral production takes a second priority to sense making; thus vocal output may not occur during this first phase. This period is also referenced to as the *silent stage* of language development.[2]

Pre-production silence can be misleading, as it can be incorrectly interpreted as an indicator of a learning or cognitive delay. Nonspeech, in a classroom setting, can be confused with an inability to understand, comprehend, or function in age-appropriate ways. It is important to keep in mind that pre-production students are almost certainly grasping and digesting much more than what their actual speaking capacity reveals.

Unlike the subsequent four stages, the pre-production *silent* phase can end abruptly. With little warning (and sometimes to great relief), a learner may virtually explode with outward speaking ability. The pre-preproduction stage is informally hallmarked by a student vocabulary of 500 words or less, and host language exposure time of approximately ten hours to eight months.

Early Production

The early production phase of learning generally occurs after the initial six months of new language exposure. During this period, students begin to entertain ownership capacities in the new language. Single word and *yes/no* responses are developed here. In addition, students are able to speak, memorize, and record repetitive beginning words and phrases. It is assumed, during the early production stage, that learners will have mastered a minimum of 1000 English words.

Speech Emergence

Speech emergence is an especially exciting stage of development, for the learner and also observing mentors. Now, a learner's vocabulary encompasses some 3,000 or more words. Most learners will embrace speech emergence following their first year of host language exposure.

During the speech emergence stage, a student grows into basic word phrasing, or clustering, capabilities. Short, patterned, and predictable sentences may be formed with little effort. Demonstrations of verbal thought streaming become more regular and complex, as the learner's familiarity with common word and sentence patterns is strengthened.

Learners routinely exude a higher level of language self-confidence at this stage. As a result, linguistic risk-taking behaviors may be spotted. These include: increased pace and frequency of speech, oral imitation, regular and recurrent teacher questioning, and social networking. This is also a critical phase in which learners begin to make essential connections between written word combinations and oral fluency.

Intermediate Fluency

Intermediate fluency presents greater challenges and opportunities for the learner. This is true because most new vocabulary acquired during this phase is content-specific. Intermediate language learners will have the comprehensive means to digest specific school subject languages, such as those used to explain math, science, or social studies.

Thus, the intermediate fluency stage typically involves a twofold responsibility on the part of the learner. He or she is expected to practice English fluency, and is meanwhile required to undertake a second dialect, which is content-specific language. Considering the complexities associated with this task, most learners will only begin to enter the intermediate fluency domain sometime after the first full year of language study. At entry, intermediate fluency students will demonstrate a manageable oral and written vocabulary of 6,000 or more English words.

Conversational language skills can appear to plateau during this time. Therefore, the intermediate stage may present itself as a period of stalemated language progress. However, any apparent pauses in this phase of language acquisition may actually be indicative of a pending breakthrough; and graduation into this penultimate stage of learning is a certain accomplishment. This new arena of content language learning calls for a recommitment to sheltered instruction and ongoing holistic support.

Continuant Language Development

With regard to English language acquisition, the Continuant Language Development (CLD) phase signals language mastery. Most students will enter the continuant sometime between their fifth and tenth year of continuous English language practice. Thus, intense patience and studious dedication are required to reach such a lofty destination on the learning continuum.

In this stage, learners possess skill sets that enable experimentation with complex functions of the English language. These include sarcasm, idioms, geographical terms and culture-specific content vocabulary, and euphemisms.

CLD students are able to use the new language on a daily conversational basis and also internally access a broad bank of vocabulary and syntax information. In short, there is an expressed ability to effectively communicate in oral and written facilities across a range of informal, academic, and professional contexts.

The CLD phase is continuant. That is, no learner's task of proficiency is ever an utterly fulfilled one. Rather, opportunities for accumulating knowledge are continuous, ongoing, and virtually limitless. The vocabulary-growth ceiling at the CLD level does not exist; it is as far-reaching as the English language itself. The level of enhanced mastery at this level depends largely upon the learner's available resources, will, and dedication.

BICS AND CALP

Basic Interpersonal Communication Skills

BICS refers to Basic Interpersonal Communication Skills. This realm pertains to basic, daily language interaction. BICS includes greetings and introductions, yes/no and simple responses, and predictable or repeated phrases (such as monetary bargaining or directional expression). BICS proficiency may be assessed formatively, through observation, engaged conversation, or written work samples. Similar processes may also be used for summative evaluation. In the latter event, tasks are more stringent and explicitly defined, and results more carefully monitored.[3]

Basic Interpersonal Communication Skills are fundamental to successful social integration. This holds true without regard to age, gender, occupation, status, or social framework. BICS skill sets can be encouraged via processes of integrating real-life scenarios with daily routine. In the context of the classroom, this might mean the following activities:

- Naming a home address and telephone number in cooperative conversation (such as Inside-Outside Circle).
- Enacting a mock goods and money exchange.
- Using facial expressions to determine a story character's feelings.
- Asking for help or bathroom permission.
- Talking through playground games or lunchtime interaction.

Cognitive Academic Language Proficiency

Cognitive Academic Language Proficiency or CALP addresses more explicit and demanding subject-specific terminology. CALP is typically associated with higher grade levels, and also with higher level thinking and application.

Generally, students require five to ten years of intense language practice before developing CALP awareness. Additional years of practice may be necessary in order to achieve proficiency.

CALP abilities are not always manifested in casual conversation, especially among peers. Rather, cognitive language skills are apt to reveal themselves in the context of advanced subjects, such as mathematics or science, wherein the content vocabulary constitutes a specific academic tongue. Linguistic specificity in this regard requires considerable practice and personal will, and therefore, may also intersect the domain of language mastery.[4]

WIDA CAN-DOS

WIDA (World-Class Instructional Design and Assessment) Can-Do descriptors provide a means for assessing student language capacities and planning for differentiated instruction for ELLs. The descriptors are portioned into grade-range clusters, encompassing pre-K through Grade 12. WIDA places emphasis on demonstrated learner ability over grade or age specification; the framework reflects this.

The WIDA rubric names four domains of language acquisition: listening, speaking, reading, and writing. Six bands of proficiency levels span the four content domains. Each numbered band details approximate skills that the learner will independently demonstrate at a given point on his or her continuum of learning.

The earliest mark on the WIDA rubric is a Level One, or *Entering*. The second band represents Level Two, or *Beginning*. These initial sections are typically reserved for the newest English language learners. Level Three (*Developing*) and Level Four (*Expanding*) provide reference points for learners who are growing and developing limited efficacy in their language abilities. Level Five, *Bridging*, illustrates sophisticated skill sets that are just under proficiency. Graduating level five indicates that the learner has achieved grade-level proficiency, or has accomplished Level Six (Reaching), and is a candidate to exit ELL programming.

Advancement through the WIDA language proficiency continuum does not necessarily correlate to a higher grade. Rather, it is an indication of proficiency across all grades. In the same way, students who are achieving at a higher tier will not necessarily require work that is at a higher grade level. We can best service our expanding and bridging learners by incorporating study that occurs at intended age or grade level, but also with deeper and more cognitively demanding purpose.

Additional information and resources related to the WIDA Can-Dos can be located on the WIDA website, located at wida.us.

THOUGHTS ON ENGLISH LANGUAGE ACQUISITION-
ENGLISH (ELA-E) RUBRICS AND ASSESSMENTS

It is important to keep in mind that a student may be academically engaged in any given combination of reading/speaking/listening levels. Significant disparities within the domains can occur at any age and at any point in the language acquisition period. For instance, a learner might present as an Early speaker, but an Intermediate reader.

Overlap is also routine. For example, learners often exhibit qualities of two or three separate proficiency levels within a single domain. In these cases, it is best to consider the area with the greatest number of indicators as the probable proficiency level. Additionally, teachers and other school personnel have the opportunity and responsibility to further customize learner evaluation through a variety of formative and summative assessment means.

LITERACY ACCESSIBILITY FOR NEWCOMER LEARNERS

Literacy, whenever possible, should be naturally imbedded in a cross-curricular capacity and should allow for readership that occurs organically and holistically. That is, opportunities for reading should be neutral and naturally occurring, and free from any rewards/punishment stipulations. In this way, we are able to capture and promote the limitless, uninhibited freedom that is the essence of literary expression and enjoyment.

Readers will read more when they are engaged; and they become engaged when they are invested in and can relate to what they are reading. What do our Newcomer students relate to? Most likely, it's the things they know. They *know* people that look and think and act in the way that they do; they *know* places that look and sound like the places they know; they *understand* intrapersonal wants and needs as they apply to their own culture, and also to the broader scope of humanity. The challenge is that those types of things are not always readily available in our classroom or school libraries.

I CAN RELATE: CELEBRATING DIVERSITY IN LITERATURE

Newcomer learners may lack access to relatable and authentic reading materials, not only in the home, but also in the school. As teachers, we consistently seek out appropriate, applicable, and enjoyable books for our learners. We seek high-quality, engaging books that students can identify with, and also texts that can be employed in a variety of teaching and learning constructs.

As teachers of Newcomers, we may be additionally motivated to incorporate worldly, informative, tolerance-boosting texts. It is likely that we have experienced some frustration in this regard. On the surface, there is a certain paucity of internationally relevant materials that teach diversity in modern, digestible ways.

Certainly, traditional core curricula have a reputation for falling short of meeting our very specific Newcomer learning needs. Essentially, most lack the structures, support, and scaffolds that make material accessible and comprehensible for ELLs. Take a moment to evaluate the text-based materials in your classroom world: reading curricula, math workbooks, science and social studies literature, and standardized tests. What do you find with regard to diversity and global perspective? What do you *wish* you could find?

It may be time to clean out, supplement, build, or revise. Relevant texts may be challenging to locate. Here are a few quality suggestions for building a multicultural library for any and all reading levels.

ABBREVIATED MULTICULTURAL BOOK LIST

ASIA

Far East

Hush: A Thai Lullaby: Minfong Ho, Holly Meade
My Face: Star Bright Books
Stone Soup: Jon J. Muth
The Name Jar Paperback: Yangsook Choi
M is For Myanmar: Elizabeth Rush, Khin Maung Myint
Grandfather's Journey: Allen Say
I Hate English: Ellen Levine
My Name is Yoon: Helen Recorvits
A Tale from Burma: Deborah Froese and Wang Kui
Throw Your Tooth on the Roof: Selby Beeler, G. Brian Karas
D is for Dragon Dance: Ying Chang Compestine
In the Snow: Huy Voun Lee
Aung San Suu Kyi: A Fearless Voice from Burma: Whitney Stewart
The Umbrella Queen: Shirin Bridges and Taeeun Yoo
Elephants of The Tsunami: Jana Laiz and Tara Cafiero
A Tale of Two Rice Birds: A Folktale from Thailand: Clare Hodgson Meeker
Buddhism in Thailand (Families & Their Faiths): Francis Hawker, et al.
Toy is from Thailand: Whitney Badgett
Children of the Dragon: Selected Tales from Vietnam: Sherry Garland and
    Trina Hyman

The Lotus Seed: Sherry Garland
Vietnam A To Z: Discover the Colorful Culture of Vietnam!: Elka K. Ra
Goodbye, Vietnam: Gloria Whelan
I See the Sun in Myanmar (Burma): Dedie King and Judith Inglese
The Wise Washerman: A Folktale from Burma: Deborah Froese and
    Wang Kui
Inside Out and Back Again: Thanhha Lai

India/Nepal

I, Doko: The Tale of a Basket: Ed Young
All the Way to Lhasa: A Tale from Tibet: Barbara Helen Berger
In Search of the Thunder Dragon: Sophie Shrestha and Romio Shrestha
The Story of a Pumpkin: A Traditional Tale from Bhutan: Tiwari, Radner,
    Rai, Adhikari
I See the Sun in Nepal: Dedie King, Judith Inglese and Chij Shrestha
N is for Nepal: Anita Adhikary
Namaste!: Diana Cohn and Amy Cordova

EAST EUROPE/WEST ASIA

Hamzat's Journey: A Refugee Diary, Anthony Robinson
A Kurdish Family (Journey Between Two Worlds): Karen O'Connor,
    Moncauskas
Russia ABCs: A Book About People and Places of Russia: Anthony Robinson
The Miraculous Child: A Christmas Folktale from Old Russia: Alvin Aleksi
    Currier
The Spider's Gift: A Ukrainian Christmas Story: Eric A. Kimmel and
    Katya Krenina
R is For Russia: Vladimir Kabakov and Prodeepta Das
The Littlest Matryoshka: Corrine Demas Bliss and Kathryn Brown
Masha and The Bear: A Story From Russia: Lori Don and Melanie
    Williamson
Radiant Girl: Andrea White
Rechenka's Eggs: Patricia Polacco
The Mitten: Jan Brett
Afghan Dreams: Young Voices of Afghanistan: Michael P. Sullivan and Tony
    O'Brien
Nasreen's Secret School: A True Story from Afghanistan: Jeanette Winter
I See the Sun in Afghanistan: Dedie King, Inglese and Vahisi
The Sky of Afghanistan: Ana A de Eulate and Sonja Wimmer

The Wooden Sword: A Jewish Folktale from Afghanistan: Ann R. Stampler, Liddiment
Words in the Dust: Trent Reedy

Middle East

The Golden Sandal: A Middle Eastern Cinderella Story: Rebecca Hickox
Mohammed's Journey (A Refugee Diary): Anthony Robinson
Kids of Kabul: Living Bravely Through a Never-Ending War: Deborah Ellis
Once Upon a Time (Seven Persian Folktales): Meimanat Mirsadeghi
Four Feet, Two Sandals: Karen Lynn Williams and Khadra Mohammed
The Best Eid Ever: Asma Mobin-Uddin and Laura Jacobsen
Silent Music: A Story of Baghdad: James Rumford
Snow in Jerusalem: Deborah da Costa
The Knight, The Princess, and the Magic Rock: A Classic Persian Tale: Sara Azizi
Pea Boy and Other Stories From Iran: Elizabeth Laird
The Earth Shook: A Persian Tale: Donna Jo Napoli
The Librarian of Basra: A True Story from Iraq: Jeanette Winter
Saving the Baghdad Zoo: A True Story of Hope and Heroes: Kelly Milner Halls, Sumner
Gilgamesh the King: Ludmila Zeman
Once Upon a Time (Severn Persian Folktales): Mirsadeghi, Meinmanat
Lebanon 1-2-3: A Counting Book in Three Languages: Marijean Boueri and Mono Trad Dabaji
Lebanon A to Z: A Middle Eastern Mosaic: Marijean Boueri and Jull Boutros
Lebanon (A World of Food): Cath Senker

AFRICA

East Africa

Beatrice's Goat: Page McBrier
Jambo Means Hello: A Swahili Alphabet Book: Muriel Feelings
We All Went on Safari: Laurie Krebs and Julia Cairns
Wangari's Trees of Peace: A True Story from Africa: Jeanette Winter
I Lost My Tooth in Africa: Penda Diakite and Baba Wague Diakite
Mama Panya's Pancakes (A Village Tale from Kenya): Rich Chamberlin and Julia Cairns
Planting the Trees of Kenya: The Story of Wangari Maathai: Claire A. Nivola
A Humble Village: Robin Joyce Miller
Christmas in Uganda: Alex Tracey and Dominique Bryon

West Africa

Chidi only Likes Blue: Ifeoma Onyefulu
A is for Africa: A Swahili Alphabet: Ifeoma Onyefulu
The Clever Monkey; A Folktale from West Africa: Rob Cleveland and Baird
    Hoffmire
Why Mosquitoes Buzz in People's Ears: A West African Tale: Verna Aardema
Zomo the Rabbit: A trickster Tale from West Africa: Gerald McDermott
The Leopard's Drum: An Asante Tale from West Africa: Jessica Souhami
Mansa Musa: The Lion of Mali: Khephra Burns and Leo & Diane Dillon
Mali Under the Night Sky: A Lao Story of Home: Youme Landowne
Why the Sky is Far Away: A Nigerian Folktale: Mary-Joan Gerson

Central/South Africa

Africa is not a Country: Margy Burns Knight and Anne Sibley O'Brien
The Magic Flyswatter: A Superhero Tale of Africa (Congo): Aaron Shepard
Who was Nelson Mandela?: Meg Belviso, Pollack, Marchesi
Nelson Mandela: Long Walk to Freedom: Chris van Wyk, Paddy Bouma
The Gift of the Sun: A Tale from South Africa: Diane Stewart and Jude Daly
Pretty Salma: A Little Red Riding Hood Story from Africa: Niki Daly
A is for Africa: Michael I. Samulak and Sswaga Sendiba
Nelson Mandela's Favorite African Folktales: Nelson Mandela
The Boy Who Harnessed the Wind: William Kamkwamba
*The Soccer Fence: A Story of Friendship, Hope and Apartheid in South
    Africa:* Phil Bildner
S is for South Africa: Beverley Naidoo and Prodeepta Das

North Africa

The Egyptian Cinderella: Shirley Climo and Ruth Heller
Brothers in Hope: The Story of the Lost Boys of Sudan: Mary Williams
Muktar and the Camels: Janet Graber
We're Sailing Down the Nile: Laurie Krebs and Anne Wilson
The Ogress and the Snake and Other Stories from Somalia: Elizabeth Laird
The Lion's Share: Said Salah Ahmed and Kelly Dupre
Wiil Waal: A Somali Folktale: retold by Kathleen Moriarty, Adam, Amir
Dhegdheer: A Scary Somali Folktale: Marian A. Hassan and Betsy Bowen
A Long Walk to Water: Based on a True Story: Linda Sue Park
Look What Came from Africa: Miles Harvey
Night Before Christmas in Africa: Foster, Christodoulou
Goal!: Mina Javaherbin

LATIN AMERICA

Federico and the Magi's Gift: A Latin American Christmas Story: Beatriz Vidal

A Mango in the Hand: A Story Told Through Proverbs: Antonio Sacre

Good-bye, Havana! Hola, New York!: Edie Colon

Coming to America: The Story of Immigration: Betsy Maestro

The Keeping Quilt Paperback: Patricia Polacco

Martina the Beautiful Cockroach: A Cuban Folktale: Carmen Agra Deedy

La Noche Buena: A Christmas Story: Antonio Sacre

Side By Side/Lado A Lado: The Story of Dolores Huerta and Cesar Chavez: Monica Brown

Esperanza Rising: Pam Munoz Ryan

My Diary from Here to There/Mi diario de aqui hasta alla: Amada Irma Perez

Pele, King of Soccer/Pele, El rey del futbol: Monica Brown

My Name is Gabriela/Me llamo Gabriela: The Life of Gabriela Mistral: Monica Brown

In My Family/En mi familia: Carmen Lomas Garza

Gracias ~ *Thanks*: Pat Mora

Biblioburro: A True Story from Columbia: Jeanette Winter

Venezuela ABCs: A Book About the People and Places of Venezuela: Katz, Cooper, Previn

The Streets are Free: Kurusa and Doppert

The Golden Flower: A Taino Myth from Puerto Rico: Nina Jaffe and Enrique O. Sanchez

Parrots Over Puerto Rico: Cindy Trumbore, Roth

The Legend of The Hummingbird: A Tale from Puerto Rico: Michael Ramirez, Sanfilippo

Juan Bobo Goes to Work: A Puerto Rican Folk Tale: Marissa Montes, Cepeda

B is For Brazil (World Alphabets): Maria de Fatimo Campos

1,2,3 Suddenly in Brazil: The Ribbons of Bonfim: Christina Falcon Maldonado, Fabrega

Dancing Turtle: A Folktale from Brazil: Pleasant DeSpain, Boston

Brazil ABCs: A Book About the People and Places of Brazil: David Seidman, Thompson

Victoria Goes to Brazil: Maria de Fatima Campos

Mariana and the Merchild: A Folk Tale from Chile: Caroline Pitcher, Morris

How Chile Came to New Mexico: Rudolfo A. Anaya, Nicolas, Nasario

Green is a Chili Pepper: A Book of Colors: Roseanne Greenfield Thong and John Parra

DIVERSITY

People: Peter Spier
What is Your Language: Debra Leventhal
One: Kathryn Otoshi
The Peace Book: Todd Parr
The Conference of the Birds: Alexis York Lumbard
One Green Apple Hardcover: Eve Bunting
Coming to America: The Story of Immigration: Betsy Maestro and Susannah Ryan
Dreaming of America: An Ellis Island Story: Eve Bunting, Stahl
Children Just Like Me: A Unique Celebration of Children Around the World: Kindersley
Whoever You are: Mem Fox, Staub
The Colors of Us: Karen Katz
The Crayon Box that Talked: Shane Derolf, Letzig
It's Okay to be Different: Christy Hale
Dreaming Up: A Celebration of Building: Christy Hale
All Families are Special: Norma Simon, Flavin
Emily and the Rainbow Umbrella: Lisl Fair, Gabot, de Polonia
All Kinds of Children: Norma Simon, Paterson
The Rainbow Stick Boy: Michael and Kate Santolini
The Family Book: Todd Parr
I'm Like You, You're Like Me: Cindy Gainer, Sakamoto
All are Family: Celebrating the Diversity of our Global Family: Bloom, Kaufman

FINAL THOUGHTS

No matter how we cut the pie, reading skills are essential. Literacy provides the essential groundwork upon which other academic, social and career frames can be constructed. Reading is a vehicle for social fluidity, professional advancement, and functional ease; and it is a conduit for mental and emotional growth. Reading and writing define people and set them apart in time and space.

Of course, as educators, we give it our all to promote healthy reading and writing skills. With every successful moment, we help generate layers of opportunity and self-efficacy in our students. We take this job seriously; and we also strive to make it fun, engaging, exciting, and memorable. We set our intentions to grow in our practice; we edit, revise, reteach, model. We celebrate in each reading victory.

Teaching literacy for Newcomer learners is absolutely inclusive of these precise aims. We just include a little extra *oomph*. We are teaching them to be competent readers in a language apart from their first. We are teaching them to become aware of their new world through text. We are guiding our learners toward future success and the ability to self-advocate via channels of literacy.

It is no small task, but it is our combined aim, nonetheless. We strive for it each day, through the most unrelenting odds. When a singular student, in a singular moment discovers achievement, our every effort is validated. When a student exclaims *in English*, "Look! I did it!" or asks, "Will you listen to me read?" we are ignited. Then, another story, in English, begins.

NOTES

1. Haynes, J., (2007). *Getting Started with English Language Learners: How Educators can Meet the Challenge*. Alexandria, VA: Association for Supervision and Curriculum Development.

2. VanPatten, B. & Benati, A.G. (2010). *Key Terms in Second Language Acquisition*. London: Continuum.

3. Cummins, J., (1981). *Empirical and Theoretical Underpinnings of Bilingual Education*. The *Journal of Education*. Vol. 163, No. 1, 16–29.

4. Loewen, S., (2004). Second Language Concerns for Refugee Children. In R. Hamilton & D. Moore (Eds.), *Educational Interventions for Refugee Children* (pp. 35–52). London: RoutledgeFalmer.

Chapter 9

Twenty-First-Century Learning

ELA-E Success in a Modern World

Bo21 La Lilemo Ho Ithuta—Sesotho

PREPARING FOR POST-SCHOOL SUCCESS

Learners who are preparing for life success in the modern world require dynamic, innovative brands of instruction. The new academic generations necessitate explicit skill sets that are separate from rote and textbook knowledge; and that ultimately promote real-world advancement. We refer to these qualifications as twenty-first century skills.

Twenty-first-century learning demands a shift away from traditional models of teaching, which tend to be very static in nature. It instead promotes the application of rigorous thinking patterns across content domains through performance-based activities, and encourages learners to effectively utilize technology and corresponding resources to achieve performance goals.

WEST MEETS EAST . . . AND SOUTH, NORTH, AND IN-BETWEEN

Twenty-first-century frameworks for instruction and learning can present certain challenges for our Newcomer populations. Namely, most non-Western educational models are structured in rote routine and memorization and tend to focus more on practical study, which may produce immediately relevant and applicable solutions for daily life. Moreover, few non-Western countries place a high emphasis on individual accomplishment or innovative gain.

Meanwhile, West-driven educational models, and particularly those in the United States, tend to be more exploratory and idiosyncratic. That is, learning aims (and teaching aims, for that matter) are perceived as distinctly individual activities. In this scenario, a single student is held highly accountable for his or her own work, and is praised or remediated according to the caliber of the work that he or she is able to produce. The Western framework, which is dependent upon individual will and gain, is in conflict with the group-success mentality that dominates most other educational landscapes.

The separate frameworks do share several distinct commonalities. First, both are reliant upon developed communication skills. Both also place high emphasis on participants' ability to work alongside peers in multiple contexts and toward a variety of shared end goals. This is the middle ground. Conveniently, interpersonal skills form a backbone for all other aspects of twenty-first-century learning. Here we have our starting point.

LAYING THE GROUNDWORK:
TWENTY-FIRST-CENTURY READINESS

Students in the twenty-first century will either be passive receptacles and storehouses of rote information or they will manipulate knowledge and ideas to create new ideas and products.[1]

A healthy twenty-first-century classroom is one that nurtures and supports active and engaged learning by providing students with as many meaningful and authentic tasks as possible throughout the school day. These opportunities to organically experience real-life learning foster creativity, problem-solving skills, and social efficacy. Authentic learning is rooted in: *(a) independent choice making; (b) opportunities for challenge; (c) a range of intrinsic and extrinsic motivational factors; and (d) connections to the self, one's learning, and the broader world context.*

Authentic tasks generate chances for growth in all areas of twenty-first-century literacy. The range and potentiality for authentic tasks in the classroom is limitless. Here we'll explore nine critical assets that will render our students among the most desirable twenty-first-century workforce candidates. They start learning them *now*, with us.

Asset 1: Innovative Communication

Communication skills form the support beams for every compiling layer of human relationships. Family, friendship, community interactions, and trade are inexplicably intertwined with communicative skills, and are also wholly dependent upon them. Effective social interchange leads to connectedness and belonging (which also happen to be key indicators for overall intrinsic happiness). Simply, *life* is something that is communicated.

So, how does this affect our students? Our Newcomer students? Essentially, they need to be prepared. They need to be able to communicate.

In the modern context, interpersonal exchange is often played out on social media and email platforms. Both of these are, in themselves, valid arenas for correspondence and demonstrate social efficacy. Communication skills are also evidenced through phone etiquette, interviewing skills, a firm handshake, or the means to compose a well-written proposal. These assets are observed at lunchroom tables, on the playground, and the respectful shift in tone when a child addresses an authority figure. Beyond these basics, students must be capable of inventing and maneuvering in much more progressive bands of exchange.

Innovative communication incorporates a fluid capacity to engage and interact with people across multiple platforms of age, race, culture, religion, language, political inclination, exposure, and experience. It involves an attuned awareness to social nuances, and an aptitude for interpersonal navigation—networking, negotiating, peacekeeping, contextual management, and appropriate expressiveness. Communication skills, essentially, are *people* skills.

Here's where this matters in the big picture: the end point for all brands of business is a consumer—a *person*. In order to produce profit, business relationships must be formed and maintained, via face-to-face contact, technological conversation, or intermediaries. Communication must pulsate through the corporate hierarchical wires; and, simultaneously, through the outstretching cords of baseline exchange.

Thus, the demand for high caliber communication abilities exists in every employable venue, at every level of operation. It follows then that our instructional efforts should match this demand in terms of providing students with authentic, organic, applicable opportunities to practise a variety of communication tactics throughout each learning day.

In fact, to some varying degree, interactive skills are *already* enforced in every academic setting, simply by the nature of the school organism. For example, students must engage with one another for a variety of purposes: establishing friendships, asking for help, collaborating with peers to problem solve, negotiating playground teams and sharing space, among other things. Young learners are also taught to interact with adults and authority figures in appropriate ways, which may be inherently dissimilar to expectations for peer interchange.

The question then becomes, how do we ensure that our students measure up? To a more pronounced degree, how do we ensure that our new-to-the-culture

ELLs stand a competitive chance in the future job market? Like everything else, we start at the beginning, and work our way up.

The beginning, in the Newcomer context, entails the careful establishment of safety and trust. It is dependent upon the meticulous fostering of individual self-confidence. It is demonstrated when we allow for multiple levels of expressive ability: oral output, drawing, labeling, singing, signing, writing, building, acting, expression or body language.

Most Newcomers enter our classrooms with underlying expertise in communication and social navigation. A majority of heritage nations place even more emphasis upon communication and community engagement than we do in the West. Not to mention, most of our students speak or understand one or more languages apart from the host tongue. We can make the most of these advantages in the classroom setting. We can begin by activating any of the communication support cues, as detailed below.

1. Let them talk. Refer back to collaborative practices . . . and let them go!
2. Limit teacher talk. The only way to really get students talking is to give them room to speak. By most figures, TTT (teacher talk time) should only account for 20%–30% of overall lesson time. Less of us, more of them.
3. Let the games begin! Small and whole group game playing encourages practical communication and strategic problem-solving skills in a non-threatening setting.
4. Model behavior. *Do* gently correct incorrect or inventive speech by repeating the question or response in the amended format.
5. Encourage descriptive speech and writing through questioning and hands-on learning.

Asset 2: Critical Thinking Capacity

Critical reasoning and critical thinking skills are among the most desirable attributes of the modern college applicant, job seeker, or entrepreneurial candidate. In fact, they are absolute prerequisites for twenty-first-century success. In the classroom, then, instruction must make way for opportunities to develop and refine critical thinking skills. Reasoning abilities are no longer purely advantageous—they are essential.

Critical reasoning employs solution-seeking strategies that can be tied to one grounding conclusion. Critical thinking skills serve a similar end, but apply higher level applications; and consequently encourage the leader to create and explore many ideas, possibilities, and opportunities. Both qualify as valuable problem-solving measures. That is, both processes demand analyzing properties and the ability to employ inductive, deductive, and/or alternative reasoning tactics as applicable.

Critical thinking and reasoning skills benefit our students in that they support balanced judgment and sound decision making. Critical reasoning invites thinkers to interpret information and conscientiously reflect upon precise predictions and decisions, thus simultaneously employing analytic and synthesizing processing. These skill sets are also intertwined with *outside-the-box* thinking, an essential component in creative solution seeking. As educators, it becomes our responsibility to endorse critical thinking and reasoning skills as viable components of twenty-first-century instruction.[2]

Asset 3: Creativity

Many modern workplaces now recognize the positive influence that creativity factors can have on overall business success. A number of companies have already established 20% rules. That is, employers set aside this amount of work time each day to allow employees space for visualization, exploration, and sharing of new ideas. If creativity is encouraged in the twenty-first-century workforce, it is certainly deserving of time and attention in the twenty-first-century classroom.

Creativity is the convergence of curiosity and problem-solving abilities. It is brought to life when humans see, feel, hear, and experience the world in original ways. Creative thinking leads to innovative ideas, which may manifest into novel designs, products, tools, solution sets, or thought output.

Creative functioning follows a predictable pattern, or a life span of thought from creation to execution.[3] The creativity platform involves three elemental steps: naming the challenge, solution seeking (problem solving) for the challenge, and defining resolution.

In life context, inventive skills will aid our students as they navigate their future lives. They fit into managing finances, negotiating travel itineraries, and coordinating college schedules. They also inspire works of art, the wording of a term paper, or a personal decision to alter a daily task for greater efficiency. Essentially, creative individuals are better equipped to meet the challenges of twenty-first-century life.

We can nurture creativity in the classroom in an infinite number of ways. We can begin by setting aside time for imaginative exploration. Inventive thinking can be further supported through cooperative talk and technology integration, where applicable. As we plan our lessons, we can be cognizant in our efforts to provide students with multiple formats in which to demonstrate efficacy and understanding. Some learners feel more inspired when soft music is playing, when they can craft, act, or sing out their thoughts, or when they are able to kinesthetically problem solve for a solution.

Mechanisms for encouraging creativity in the classroom are also indicators for sheltered instruction. That is, we very likely nudge our students' imagination as an existing byproduct of the Newcomer instruction model. If we consider creativity as an essential twenty-first-century virtue, then we can be inspired to (creatively!) continue and expand upon our efforts to reinforce these skills.

Asset 4: Flexibility

Flexibility is demonstrated by an individual's capacity to accept and adapt to change. These particular skill sets are usually situational; and thus are influenced by time, variable outcome, artistic influence, personality, feedback, negotiation, and other sensitivities. They are essential twenty-first-century competencies.

Flexibility carries various faces and weights. It can mean adjusting to variant schedules and routines; adapting to shifting roles, such as weekly changes in classroom job assignments; or the ability to digest and respond to both positive and negative feedback. Ultimately, this form of intrapersonal dexterity is a reflection of a person's capacity to cope with unpredictability and other unknowns.[4]

For our Newcomers, flexibility can carry a pronounced load. Our learners must adapt at extreme levels to situations that may be *entirely* new. Newcomers may be experts in flexibility long before they reach our classrooms. Many have learned to make creative adjustments when predicted food sources are not available; when *home* takes on a very mobile meaning; when loss and uncertainty occurs; and when financial resources exist as ebb and flow commodities.

Nonetheless, structure and stability are of essential value to our Newcomers. Stability and predictability are markers of security. As a result, that 11 a.m. fire drill in the middle of math could disrupt the entire remaining portion of the school day, as students may be unable to recapture their original focus and concentration. School breaks may trigger panic, anxiety, and temper tantrums. The effects of one substitute teacher day may be felt for two weeks.

Preparing our students for twenty-first-century success means making room for opportunities to practise flexibility, but with safety nets in place. This can be accomplished by occasionally shifting reading group compositions, or by reversing the order of learning stations for a day. It sometimes helps to create the shift for something fun and memorable, such as an outside scavenger hunt during a scheduled block, or hosting unannounced reading buddies for an afternoon.

In any event, our students need to know flexibility. Or, as is the case for most of our Newcomer students, revisit the skill. Why? Because their future lives and workplaces will demand it. So, we are not doing our charges any favors by leaving flexibility out of the school day.

We, as teachers, are absolutely expected to practice flexibility. We practically exude it, because no part of our day is predictable. Ever. If the best recipe is to teach what you know, then we are bona fide experts in this category!

Asset 5: Self-Initiative

Initiative is a character trait highly prized by employers. It's a good trait to have on your resume. It's what separates the leaders from the doers.[5]

Self-initiative calls for independent goal setting, as well as the ability to effectively prioritize, monitor, and manage time, learning, and productivity. This family of skill sets is grounded in self-regulation, self-management, and strategic ownership. Self-initiating learners find direction with limited outside prompting, and are inspired to continuously develop in a target area or areas. As a whole, self-initiation strengths are key indicators for future success in twenty-first-century professional work environments.[6]

Self-directive traits in the classroom context can manifest in a variety of ways, all of which are grounded in personal investment. They include the urgency to track scores and set independent improvement goals; to voluntarily assume necessary communal roles and duties; or to self-assess based on a familiar rubric. Self-evaluative forms of accountability usually take visible root by the fourth grade. With guidance, these skills mature into the high school learning years and beyond.

Self-initiative is closely linked with motivation, and specifically intrinsic incentive. Healthy intrapersonal motivation is also linked to a high IQ and overall life achievement. In short, self-initiative and factors of motivation can be hugely influential in terms of determining immediate and long-term triumphs of our students.[7] With regard to our Newcomer students, self-initiative can also enhance the possibility for timely and vigorous integration into the host society.

In the aim of fostering self-initiation skills, we can begin by offering learners a range of learning materials to pique a spectrum of interests. Next, we can aid students in naming and understanding a baseline data point for a specific aim, such as math facts competency. We then offer similar guidance in identifying a goal point (advanced students can provide reasoning and explanation). Throughout the goal-seeking process, our task is to mentor students in record keeping (such as graphing score values weekly).

Essentially, the best thing we can do is to set our students up and then get out of the way. We reteach and remind as necessary. We praise gains. More than this, we praise unyielding efforts as efforts in any regard, and we celebrate them as incredible opportunities for new understanding and growth. Our mindfulness to these basic foundations helps us guide our students as they evolve from *reactive* to *proactive* participants in learning, and ultimately, develop as self-initiating individuals.[8]

Asset 6: Leadership Skills

Leadership skills involve persuading others toward the accomplishment of a specific aim or aims, meanwhile exercising integrity, ethical maturity, interpersonal skills, strategic problem solving, and awareness for the common good.[9] We strive to promote these skills in the school because they aid our children in developing positive human character, and also because we understand that businesses favor candidates with strong leadership skills as a means of enhancing bottom line and company productivity.

In as much as leadership entails guiding, it must also encompass diplomacy, fairness, and equity. True leaders bear in mind the best interests of the whole, and they comprehend the divergence between imperiousness and spirited, pragmatic headship. Opportunities to exercise leadership in the school setting should be governed by parameters of equity and accountability, virtues that should also be modeled by adult guides.[10]

In the classroom setting, leadership skills are fostered through interactive activities that include project planning, team building, time and project management, goal setting, problem solving, and diversity awareness.[11] Essentially, chances to practice leadership skills are prevalent in settings where other twenty-first-century skill sets are already evident.

In fact, the leadership facet is unique in that it may be directly applied to all other faculties of twenty-first-century development. It has a capacity to enhance or diminish the efficacy of any area where it is applied. The school setting, with all its safety nets in place, is an ideal ground for testing, modifying, and strengthening healthy leadership abilities.

Asset 7: Accountability and Productivity

Accountability and productivity are two separate twenty-first-century functions that are irrefutably linked to one another. In short, these skill sets require that individuals work hard, work effectively, and take responsibility for their work. Demonstrated strengths in the arenas of accountability and productivity lend themselves to success in the classroom; and they are all but a guaranteed precondition for post-graduation hiring.

Productivity entails envisioning a goal, and then implementing the specific procedures and protocol necessary to ensure completion of the overall task or objective. The process demands preplanning, careful management of time and physical resources, the ability to work under pressure and satisfy deadlines, and a willingness to accept and grow from positive and negative feedback. Accountability is the ownership piece. Accountable individuals demonstrate a sense of duty and proprietorship for their work and personal choices. This is where the doing and the character of the doer meet.

Accountability and productivity skills are most effective when they are employed in conjunction with other essential skill sets, such as creativity and collaboration. This makes them a perfect fit for the classroom, where partnership traits are ubiquitous. Accountability and productivity skills are also encouraged through collaborative exchange, which we already strive to nurture as a part of our respectful learning community.

Clear objectives and carefully defined rubrics guide learners toward productivity and self-accountability (picture rubrics are appropriate for Newcomers). When students know exactly what is expected of them, they are more equipped to achieve the higher goal. Diminished teacher talk time allows students to get to work quickly, and sentence stems lay the ground-work for on-task talk. Brain breaks provide fresh blood flow and stimulate focus energy (we love GoNoodle!). Making room for appropriate technology input saves time and develops expertise. Involving parents can also deeply enhance students' accountability and productivity aims.

Productivity and accountability are evidenced in every imaginable facet of the workforce. They should be evidenced in every arena of our classroom, beginning with our example. We, alongside our students, are all part of the same team. We work hard together, receive feedback together, and grow together. We do it, we own it, we refine it; and we achieve.

Asset 8: Civic Duty and Social Fluidity

Civic Education in a democracy is education in self-government.[12]

Civic fluency enables our young people to become diligent, constructive contributors within our communal landscapes, and also in the global com-posite. Civic engagement and social maneuverability skills are fundamental components of twenty-first-century learning. They are also at the root of social participation.

Civic competencies involve a cognizance of social structure and policy. Competency in this realm invokes an understanding of personal choices and liberties that are available under a given civil framework, as well as the duties and obligations that define good citizenship. We can count on the reality that our current students will inevitably become the decision makers of our future. There are substantial reasons to guide them well!

One source writes that, "The availability of a knowledgeable and skilled citizenry will enhance the quality of life and result in a profitable economy for [our state], our nation, and our world."[13] Who better to prepare young people for successful civic engagement than those of us who spend so much time crafting, enabling, and empowering our charges each school day? The fact is, schools possess an unmatched capacity for imparting civic awareness and gainful social duty.

Our role is doubly profound in the Newcomer setting. These young learners and their families are the freshest contributors to the vibrant American landscape; slivers in the kaleidoscope that is our wondrous nation. Imagine the utter sense of newness that many Newcomers experience in their first encounters with the host environment. Consider the potentially overwhelming weight of cultural novelty, and the understandable chasms in accurate background knowledge of the host country.

Customs, expectations, holidays, and citizenship protocol in the host democracy setting must be absorbed, learned, and embraced. It is a lot to soak in. In any case, Newcomer students simply *will* be expected to make sense of how to get along, abide by rules, and become accountable citizens. Our young Newcomers might also be responsible for transferring an awareness of basic laws and citizenship frameworks to adult family members. At least, they will be expected to make discoveries about their roles as citizens in the new country alongside their adult counterparts.

Civic learning in the classroom occurs through direct instruction about the government, governmental leaders and history, and normative social values of the host nation. It is also taught through modeling of essential platforms, such as democratic participation. Civic dispositions, which encompass character virtues, are also teachable. These include moral responsibility, integrity, self-discipline, respect, ability to compromise, empathy, dedication to obeying laws, and a cognizance of human interconnectedness.[14]

In the classroom setting, we can spur these skills by encouraging learners to become involved in the community through volunteer service or interviewing. Creating a classroom city, government and/or court are also beneficial exercises. Younger students can design character maps of a good citizen, give news reports or conduct relevant author studies (Eve Bunting is a great choice!).

Ultimately, students need to be able to use what they know in order to evaluate circumstances, engage in critical thinking skills, and become active, informed decision makers in the civic realm.[15] It is possible—and fun—to incorporate civic literacy into routine learning in authentic, meaningful ways, at every age and language ability level. Of course, we will continue to model the great citizenship attributes that we hope to see in our students. This is our very unique civic duty!

Asset 9: Technology Literacy

As twenty-first-century educators, we are expected to participate in various technical applications related to our field, and simultaneously equip learners to become adept future manipulators of technological resources. The incorporation of technology is exponentially vital in the Newcomer context; and it may also be complicated, as we often assume the task of *introducing* children and families to modern resources. In any event, our students must enjoy some ownership of technological mastery in order to fully contribute to a modern society.

How do we integrate technology in our classroom and at our school? How could we increase and expand upon learners' opportunities to employ technology in their educational processes? How do we define, model, and hold students accountable for issues of ethics regarding technology and digital information?

MAKING {VIRTUAL} ROOM: DIGITAL GAMING AS A BEST PRACTICES APPROACH

There is an evident push in the twenty-first century to incorporate educational gaming into our traditional pedagogical systems. These efforts are in place not to serve as replacements for direct instruction, but to act as viable supplements with the capacity to enhance everyday classroom and home learning programs. Games-based learning has a demonstrated capacity to motivate learners, activate knowledge acquisition, and enhance critical thinking capacities. When employed and monitored responsibly, digital game exposure and manipulation can support and empower users in learning and future employment endeavors.[16–18]

Technological gaming has more in common with traditional educational structures than we might realize. In fact, the overlap is significant. There are definite similarities to sheltered instruction classrooms. Namely, games (like sheltered instruction techniques) allow for personalized, leveled means of differentiated instruction and assessment that are not language limited. Here we'll explore these and other shared factors.

Play

Kids are so inherently, wholly *good* at it. They run, jump, flick paper clips, and spin pencils. They play, they seek joy . . . and they don't really care who's watching. Games are the most prevalent kind of play, and arguably the most fun. Video game designers realized the significance of play; it is the cornerstone of their craft. Schools also recognize the power of play, and we cater to it in a broad spectrum of ways.

Nearly all games rely upon positive peer interchange as a prerequisite for their existence, and relationship building is almost universally promoted throughout the game's entire timeline. They also allow participants the *choice* to be involved in an activity in which they are intrinsically interested in. They provide opportunities for players to demonstrate specific strengths, to coach others, and to become mentees themselves in safe, nonthreatening arenas.

Central Goal

Goals are the defining point of separation between play and a game. Well-designed programs offer a clear and attractive end goal, as well as imbedded mini-goals. Comparatively, well-developed classroom frameworks offer specific, achievable end goals, strengthened by the integration of ongoing, identifiable mini-goals. Many games, especially serious games, establish an overlap between goal setting and achievement in gaming, and goal setting and real-life efforts.[19,20]

Rules

The rules of play, implicit or overt, act as the architecture for all forms of game design. Rules-design adheres to the principle that rule followers will progress through the game cycle, while game play for those who misunderstand or attempt to undermine the established rules framework will be delayed or ended. Rule structures should be clear, concise, and well communicated; and they should be tied to swift and appropriate consequences for the player's conscious choice to align or disengage from an established rules framework. Rule structures apply to virtually every arena of life, and are especially evidenced in the school setting.

Feedback

Feedback is a fundamental component of gaming. It is also vital to every academic and professional function. A feedback loop begins when the participant voluntarily completes an action, which stimulates a system response (feedback). The participant interprets the feedback information and reacts accordingly, eliciting a fresh system response. The participant commits to a rejoinder, and the loop is extended until the game has reached an endpoint, or until the participant voluntarily terminates the loop.[21]

Of course, we teachers already *know* about feedback. We emit feedback for shoe tying, line walking, bathroom noise making, vowel skipping, subtractive borrowing, and homework missing. We receive feedback for our cumulative test scores, our evaluated performance . . . and, from our students, for our hair choices, coffee breath, and story selections. We grade homework, we conference with our students over their writing, and we engage behavior modification systems.

The difference is that technological feedback loops are direct and instantaneous with a wholly interactive and experience-based set of perimeters and guideposts.[22] The user moves, the game responds. The student moves, we respond as teachers—just not nearly as quickly. Students thrive when feedback is hastened. Intrinsic motivation balloons, and learning is amplified exponentially. It is possible for us to share *some* of our feedback responsibilities with technology in ways that significantly benefit our learners!

Voluntary Participation

This is the only component of gaming that strays from most school and professional duties. This missing ingredient equates to a devastating void in our school and employment frameworks. Why? Well, because voluntary participation is the key holder to *fun*. By the simple act of choice, any activity, including learning, is magnificently enhanced. When personal choice is introduced, positive work outcomes such as productivity, accuracy, and motivation correspondingly increase.[23]

Personalization

Digital games are programmed to *read* us, the users. They must accurately capture an overview of a player's current level of expertise and projected wants and needs, and then adapt play to match the changing analyses. Well-designed games engage pertinent measures of scaffolding through a skeleton of levels, and intensify in correlation with the user's skill evolution. It is probable, as we move into the future, that personalized learning will become a more conjoined effort between the digital screen and the hands-on teacher. We can ease into the processes sooner, or later.[24,25]

Removed Fear of Failure

Gaming is structured on the premise that a user directly owns the right to not pass; and each player is also afforded infinite opportunities to *try again*. Players (aka game learners) appear to thrive in this kind of full-spectrum arena, wherein mistakes become synonymous with new prospects. In this unique setting, wrong paths equate to little more than turn-around points in the cognitive problem-solving processes; and personal advancement is derived from a true understanding of pattern, function, and reason. Ultimately, *failure* becomes obsolete. Without the failure component, shame has no alternative but to dissolve.[26]

Community Building

Virtual gaming, like other forms of interaction, lends itself to collaboration and community building. In the simplest form, humans have a natural tendency to form bonds with those who share similar interests. Relationships are further strengthened when the commonalities are also sources of joy and entertainment. Meanwhile, sense of belonging and teamwork are an output of situations that require converging energies to achieve a mutual, higher outcome. Conveniently, fun is one of our most prized human facilitators of positive communication. Games are one embodiment of this.

Assessment

Essentially, all technology-based games are also assessments. That is, they recognize, evaluate, and rank the quality of participatory effort. Games also adjust accordingly so as to promote challenging, yet enjoyable, ongoing user responses.

In the gaming world, assessments are malleable. They can easily adapt to offsets in participatory understanding, and are routinely modified in accordance with user ability. Digital games grow in complexity along with the participant as he or she becomes more adept in the targeted skill areas. Any user evaluation data that may be gleaned from gaming constructs is pertinent in terms of guiding next steps, which in gaming constructs equates to continued practice, or *leveling up*.[27]

Many schools now utilize data gleaned from student gaming efforts as respectable gauges for status and growth in a variety of faculties. Namely, students' educational gaming statistics can lend valuable insight regarding initial learner placement, real growth, and forecasted trajectories of development. The same information lends itself to effective, informed instructional planning. In the Newcomer realm, the digitally interactive *Imagine Learning English* is one example of this.

Of course, with regard to digital assessments, most school and state tests have also already breached the cusp from pencil-and-paper to online versions. The digital assessment shift is not coming; it is already here. Virtual gaming has occupied center field in this progression, and it continues to maintain its post as the MVP of instantaneous, evaluative schematics. At some point in the trajectory of educational best practices, we will be required to wholly internalize the value of gaming as a reliable tool for assessment.

Debriefing

Debriefing is the thoughtful, purposeful reflection on one's experience, which is enhanced through relevant social interchange. This process should follow education game play, as a conduit for a complete circuit of understanding. Most debriefing occurs as a natural activity. In the classroom context, debriefing may be guided and modeled, and can occur through speech, writing, or other expressive means.[28,29]

SERIOUS SIMULATION GAMES

We believe these exciting world-class tools have the potential to fundamentally change the way students and teachers interact in the classroom, and ultimately, how education works in America.—Vicki L. Phillips at the Bill & Melinda Gates Foundation.[30]

FOUNDATION, ON SERIOUS GAMES

Serious Simulation Games are games that are designed for the fundamental purposes of education for reaching a solution for real-world dilemmas.[31,32] Some serious simulation games are:

- *United Nations Food Force:* Players, as a collaborative whole, must determine the best and fairest means of allocating goods and resources, according to a wide range of factors.
- *Fold It:* Users participate alongside actual researchers in solving a number of complex protein-structure puzzles, which translate into real-time research. Points are earned for correct manipulation of amino acid strands.
- *Celestia:* Players create realities and solve dilemmas specific to the course of elected real-time simulation within a three-dimensional, interactive space exploration experience.
- *Planet Hunters*: Users manipulate the Kepler public archives in collaborative simulation star quests. Actual researchers carefully analyze players' astrological observations. 12 million observations of 43 planet candidates have been recorded to date.[33]
- *Armchair Revolutionary*: Players participate in purposeful social engagement. User success is contingent upon global collaboration, and is corroborated by the organized integration of real-world opportunities to apply virtual content.
- *MineCraft:* Players strategically break and assemble blocks, all in an effort to devise structures that protect from nocturnal creatures. Over time, it

has evolved into an intensely collaborative and creative platform for user design, imagination, architectural resolve, problem solving, reasoning, strategic policy, social understanding, and relationship building. Applications are cross-curricular.

- *MiniMonos:* Players from around the world work together to navigate a web of eco issues via their monkey avatars. The avatars socialize with one another, collectively brainstorm, and collaboratively seek out and act on conservation solutions across a selection of mini games.

Alternative interactive educational programming:

Early Ages (2–6):

- Endless Ocean
- Reader Rabbit
- LeapFrog Leapster
- Professor Layton Series
- LittleBigPlanet
- Shiny Bakery (number sense, practical skills)
- Math Elements (early math skill practice)
- Playnormous (health and wellness education)
- Mingoville (English language learning for kids)
- English Attack!
- LearnEnglishKids
- PBS Kids (variety of early/mid-level learning games)
- ABC Mouse (variety of early/mid-level puzzles and games)
- YA Games
- StarFall (variety of early/mid-level learning games)
- CoolMathGames (variety of early/mid-level learning games)
- Magic School Bus

Middle Years (7–12):

- Whyville (interactive broad-based education)
- Plan-It Commander (openly addresses the realities and needs of ADHD learners)
- Monkey Quest (math skills focus)
- Word Raider (vocabulary skills practice)
- Power Up (science/environment with special disabilities accommodations)
- What to Learn (educational mini games)
- Forestia (forest/resource management simulation)
- Freedom: The Underground Railroad (virtual, cooperative strategizing)
- WolfQuest (science and nature)

- ElectroCity (energy, conservation, urban planning)
- eLECTIONS (introductory interactive politics, presidential hopeful role-play)
- Super Smart Games (diverse educational subjects)
- Nobel Prize Educational Games (diverse educational subjects)
- Thinking Worlds (diverse educational subjects)
- SimCityEdu (environment, policy, collaboration)
- Refraction (animal rescue, space travel)
- Scribblenauts
- Civilization

Advanced (13+):

- A Force More Powerful (Solving world conflict through nonviolent methods)
- Oinkonopolis (economics and civil skills)
- Bonds Training (financial literacy and stock market simulation)
- SpaceChem Darfur is Dying (social conflict resolution, global awareness)
- Betwixt Folly and Fate (civil war history and historical life simulation)
- FloodSim (A flood and flood prevention interactive simulation game)
- NanoQuest (mini adventures in physics, chemistry, and biology)
- 3rd World Farmer (cooperative strategy game addressing Africa-specific needs, also in Spanish)
- World Without Oil (natural resources awareness, crisis shortage simulation)
- Robo Rush (financial literacy and business strategy)
- Blended Learning for Science and Social Studies
- Kids.USA.Gov (social studies/science)
- Ology (science/social studies)
- Go North! (science)
- The JASON Project (science/social studies)
- The GLOBE Program (science/social studies)
- Journey North (science)
- NASA Quest (science)
- Science Kids (science)
- Place the States (geography)
- Strike it Rich (social studies/history)

Virtual Field Trips

- Colonial Williamsburg Electronic Field Trip—American history
- Scholastic Plymouth Plantation Virtual Field Trips—American history
- Smithsonian Museum—world history and art

- Inside The Whitehouse—politics, American government
- 4-H Virtual Farm—rural life, life cycles, animal viewing
- Explore The Estuary—waves, tides, oceans
- Virtual Geographic Field Trip To Griffith Park—earthquakes, landforms, tectonics

FINAL THOUGHTS

Our students will be expected to achieve proficiency in every facet of modern functionality, from technological fluency to civic duty to social maneuverability. In direct correspondence, we, the educators, will also be held accountable to motivate, empower, and enrich our students to the extent that they are able to meet the expectations of the twenty-first-century framework, and thrive in adult productivity arenas.

NOTES

1. Cash, Richard M, Ed.D (2010). *Advancing Differentiation: Thinking and Learning for the 21st Century.* Free Spirit Publishing.

2. Cash, Richard M, Ed.D (2010). *Advancing Differentiation: Thinking and Learning for the 21st Century.* Free Spirit Publishing.

3. Lai, Emily R. (2011). Critical Thinking: A Literature Review. *Research Report.* Pearson Publishing. Located at images.pearsonassessments.com/images/ tmrs/CriticalThinkingReviewFINAL.pdf. Retrieved Feb, 2015.

4. Cash, Richard M, Ed.D (2010). *Advancing Differentiation: Thinking and Learning for the 21st Century.* Free Spirit Publishing.

5. Trilling, Bernie and Charles Fadel (2007). *21st Century Skills: Learning For Life In Our Times* (1st Ed). Jossey-Bass.

6. Partnerships for 21st Century Learning (2009). *P21 Framework Definitions.* Located at p21.org. Retrieved July 2011.

7. Lai, Emily R. (2011). Critical Thinking: A Literature Review. *Research Report.* Pearson Publishing. PDF locate at images.pearsonassessments.com/images/ tmrs/CriticalThinkingReviewFINAL.pdf. Retrieved Feb. 2015.

8. Van Briesen, Jeanne M. (2009). Oral presentation for Department of Civil and Environmental Engineering Carnegie Mellon University. Located at nae.edu. Retrieved May 2015.

9. Partnerships for 21st Century Learning (2009). *P21 Framework Definitions.* Located at p21.org. Retrieved July 2011.

10. Cash, Richard M, Ed.D (2010). *Advancing Differentiation: Thinking and Learning for the 21st Century.* Free Spirit Publishing.

11. Hay, I., & Dempster, N. (2004). Student Leadership Development within a School Curriculum Framework. In Bartlett, B., Bryer, F., & Roebuck, D. (Eds)

Education: *Weaving Research into Practice*. International Language, Cognition and Special Education Conference, Gold Coast Vol. 2, 141–50.

12. Branson, Margaret S. (1989). *International and Citizenship Education: Need and Nexus*. Paper presented at the International Conference on Constitutional Government and the Development of an Enlightened Citizenry, Los Angeles, CA. ED 314 302.

13. Iowa Department of Education (2010). *Iowa Core K-12 21st Century Skills: Essential Concepts and Skills with Details and Examples*. Located at https://www. educateiowa.gov/sites/files/ed/documents/K-12_21stCentSkills_0.pdf. Retrieved May 2014.

14. Branson, Margaret S. (1989). *International and Citizenship Education: Need and Nexus*. Paper presented at the International Conference on Constitutional Government and the Development of an Enlightened Citizenry, Los Angeles, CA. ED 314 302.

15. Cain, Jim, Michelle Cummings & Jennifer Stanchfie (2005). *A Teachable Moment: A Facilitator's Guide to Activities for Processing, Debriefing, Reviewing and Reflection* (1st Ed). Kendall Hunt Publishing.

16. McGonigal, Jane (2011). *Reality Is Broken: Why Games Make Us Better and How They Can Change the World* (1st Ed). Penguin Press.

17. Jacobson, Elle (2014). *Research Roundup: Studies Support Game-based Learning*. Located at https://www.filamentgames.com/research-roundup-studies-support-game-based-learning. Retrieved Feb 2015.

18. Breuer, Bente (2010). Eludamos, *Journal for Computer Game Culture*. Vol. 4 No. 1, 7–24.

19. Kapp, Karl M. (2013). *Goals in Learning: The Gamification of Learning and Instruction*. Pfeiffer Publishing.

20. Shelton, Brett E. & Jon Scoresby (2011). *Aligning Game Activity with Educational goal: Following a Constrained Design Approach to Instructional Computer Games*. Utah. Located at Educational Technology Research and Development. Retrieved October 2012.

21. Thompson, Debbie, et al. (2012). In Pursuit of Change: Youth Response to Intensive Goal Setting Embedded in a Serious Video Game. *J Diabetes Sci Technol*. 2007; 1: 907–17.

22. McGonigal, Jane (2011). *Reality is Broken: Why Games Make Us Better and How They Can Change the World* (1st Ed). Penguin Press.

23. McGonigal, Jane (2011). *Reality Is Broken: Why Games Make Us Better and How they can Change the World* (1st Ed). Penguin Press.

24. McClarty, et al. (2012). *A Literature Review of Gaming Education*. Pearson Publishing.

25. Sander Bakkes, Check Tien Tan & Yusuf Pisan (2012). *Personalised Gaming: A Motivation and Overview of Literature*. New Zealand: Auckland, Located at sander. landodsand/publications. Retrieved Aug 2015.

26. McClarty, et al. (2012). *A Literature Review of Gaming Education*. Pearson Publishing.

27. Breuer, Bente (2010). *Eludamos* Journal for Computer Game Culture. Vol. 4 No. 1, 7–24.

28. Fanning Ruth M. & David M. Gaba (2007). *The Role of Debriefing in Simulation Based Learning.* University Medical School at Stanford, Vol. 2, No 2.

29. Cain, Jim, Michelle Cummings & Jennifer Stanchfie (2005). *A Teachable Moment: A Facilitator's Guide to Activities for Processing, Debriefing, Reviewing and Reflection* (1st Ed). Kendall Hunt Publishing.

30. Bill and Melinda Gates Foundation (2015). *Press Release: Gates Foundation Announces Portfolio of Innovative Grants to Develop New Teaching and Learning Tools that Support Teachers and Help Students.* Located at gatesfoundation.org. Retrieved June 2015.

31. Ulisack, Mary (2010). *Games in Education: Serious Games.* Future Lab UK. Located at media.futurelab.org.uk/resources/documents/lit_reviews/Serious-Games_ Review.pdf. Retrieved July 2, 2015.

32. Gates, Bill. Written testimony of Bill Gates before Committee on Science and Technology, U.S. House of Representatives: http://www.sciencedebate2008.com/ www/index.php?id=27.

33. Wang, Ji (PhD) (2014). *Planet Hunters, A Zooniverse Project Blog.* Located at http://blog.planethunters.org/category/planets. Retrieved June 2014.

Closing Thoughts

The landscape of Newcomer education is vast and varied. It is a place for the cross-germination between modern Western academic standards and international elements of language, culture, and custom. In this terrain, whole worlds come together. Some of us just call it our classroom.

As educators, Newcomer instruction presents us with exceptional challenges. We are challenged to communicate across a multitude of heritage languages, facilitate cultural integration and address manifestations of trauma and transition shock. Beyond this, we are faced with the task of differentiating learning in imaginative and innumerable ways.

In ways that trump the offsets of the profession, Newcomer education also provides teachers with compelling opportunities for personal and professional transformation. We are very often our students' first established trust-based relationship in the host country. We might just be the first smile, the first hug, and the first attempt at direct eye contact with an adult in the new setting.

From our very unique perspectives, we are capable of impacting learner lives in incredibly profound ways. In the process, we help to define, model, and encourage positive citizenry in the host environment. We become more than teachers—we become pillars of stability, welcoming, and ultimately, knowledge.

The demographic that we teach to is exceptional. Our approaches to instruction and interaction with students and families must be equally exceptional. When we provide our Newcomer students with the cultural, linguistic, and physiological tools that they need, we can begin to anticipate social and academic growth. We can begin to reach for greatness.

We start one piece at a time, one foot in front of the other. We start with teaching a student how to hold a pencil, how to shake hands, and how to express their most basic needs, wants, and feelings. We create safe foundations and build upward by sheltering and scaffolding instruction, and by providing rigorous multicultural learning opportunities. We choose to be present and deliberate in our craft each and every day.

Our Newcomer students, with time, will develop their capacities in the host setting. They will showcase their resiliency, ingenuity, and determination in the most remarkable ways. In as much as we are responsible for imparting academic truths and promoting discovery, our students also leave us with important world lessons and life-affirming insights. Optimally, educators and Newcomer students grow alongside one another, in a cooperative exchange of experience, knowledge, and global understanding. When we enable this model to occur, we define and exemplify the very essence of our teaching craft.

Appendix I

Elementary English Homonym List

AIR–ERE–ERR–HEIR
AISLE–I'LL–ISLE
ALLOWED–ALOUD
ANT–AUNT
ATE–EIGHT
AYA–EYE–I

BAND–BANNED
BARE–BEAR
BERRY–BURY
BE–BEE
BEAT–BEET
BUY–BY–BYE
BLEW–BLUE
BREAD–BRED
BRAKE–BREAK

CAPITAL–CAPITOL
CEDE–SEED
CEILING–SEALING
CELL–SELL
CHANCE–CHANTS
CHEAP–CHEEP
CLOSE–CLOTHES
COARSE–COURSE
CREAK–CREEK
CENT–SENT
CYMBAL–SYMBOL

DAYS–DAZE
DEAR–DEER

DEW–DO
DIE–DYE
DISCUSSED–DISGUST
DOE–DOUGH
DUAL–DUEL

EAVE–EVE
ERN–EARN–URN
EXERCISE–EXORCISE
EWE–YEW–YOU

FIR–FUR
FEAT–FEET–FETE
FAIRY–FERRY
FAIR–FARE
FLEA–FLEE
FLEW–FLU–FLUE
FLOUR–FLOWER
FOUL-FOWL

GAIT–GATE
GNU–KNEW–NEW
GORRILLA–GUERRILLA
GROAN–GROWN
GUESSED–GUEST

HAIR–HARE
HALVE–HALF
HAY–HEY
HALL–HAUL
HEAL–HEEL

HEAR–HERE
HI–HIGH
HIGHER–HIRE
HOLE–WHOLE
HOARSE–HORSE
HOUR–OUR

IDLE–IDOL
IN–INN
ITS–IT'S

KNOT–NOT
KNOWS–NOSE
KNOW–NO
KNEAD–NEED
KNIGHT–NIGHT

LEAD–LED
LEAK–LEEK
LOAN–LONE

MAID–MADE
MAIL–MALE
MAIN–MANE
MAIZE–MAZE
MANNER–MANOR
MARRY–MERRY
MALL–MAUL
MEAT–MEET–METE
MEDAL–MEDDLE
METAL–METTLE
MISSES–MRS.
MORNING–MOURNING

NAVAL–NAVEL
NEED–KNEAD
NONE–NUN

ONE–WON
OAR–OR–ORE–O'ER
ODE–OWED

PAIL–PALE
PAIN–PANE
PAIR–PARE–PEAR

PASSED–PAST
PAUSE–PAWS
PEACE–PIECE
PEDAL–PEDDLE–PETAL
PEAK–PEEK–PIQUE
PEER–PIER
PI–PIE
PLAIN-PLANE
PRINCIPAL–PRINCIPLE
PRESENCE–PRESENTS
PORE–POUR
PRAY–PREY
POLE–POLL

RAIN–REIGN–REIN
READ-RED
READ–REED
RAISE–RAZE–RAYS
RAP–WRAP
REAL–REEL
RESIDENCE–RESIDENTS
RING–WRING
ROAD–ROWED
ROLE–ROLL
ROOT–ROUTE
ROSE–ROWS
ROUGH–RUFF

SACS–SACKS–SAX
SAIL–SALE
SEAM–SEEM
SEAS–SEES–SEIZE
SEW–SO–SOW
SIGHED–SIDE
SIGHT–SITE
SHONE–SHOWN
SLAY–SLEIGH
SOAR–SORE
SOME–SUM
SOOT–SUIT
STAIR–STARE
STEAL–STEEL
STRAIGHT–STRAIT
SUNDAE–SUNDAY

TACKED–TACT
TACKS–TAX
TEAS–TEASE–TEES
TEAR–TIER
TEAM–TEEM
THEIR–THERE–THEY'RE
TIDE–TIED
TO–TOO–TWO
TOAD–TOED–TOWED

VAIN-VEIN-VANE
VIAL–VILE

WADE–WEIGHED
WALK–WOK
WAIL–WHALE

WAIST–WASTE
WAIT–WEIGHT
WAIVE–WAVE
WAR–WORE
WARE–WEAR–WHERE
WEAK–WEEK
WEATHER–WHETHER
WE'D–WEED
WE'LL–WHEEL
WHICH–WITCH
WOOD–WOULD

YOKE–YOLK
YOU'LL–YULE
YOUR–YOU'RE

Appendix II

International Tongue Twisters

Khait hareer ala hait Im khaleel. *A silk thread on Khaleel's wall.—Arabic*

Buổi trưa ăn bưởi chua. *Having pomelos for lunch.—Vietnamese*

El bebé bebe bebidas. *The baby drinks sodas.—Spanish*

Ái á Á, á á í á. *Grandfather from "Á" farm has a sheep in a river. —Icelandic*

Kachaa paapaD, pakkaa paapaD. *Cooked lentil wafer, raw lentil wafer —Hindi*

Kartal kalkar dal sarkar, dal sarkar kartal kalkar. *The eagle takes off, the branch bends; the branch bends, the eagle takes off.—Turkish*

Mái mai mài mài chài mái. *New silk doesn't burn, does it?—Thai*

Três tristes tigres. *Three sad tigres—Portugese*

Roukhi we roukhik ya roukhi roukhain be roukh matrakh ma troukh roukhik roukhi bet roukh! *My soul and your soul are one soul. Wherever your soul goes, my soul also goes!*

Lặt rau rồi luộc. *Cut and boil the vegetables.—Vietnamese*

Škof v škaf skoči. *The bishop jumps into a tub.—Slovenian*

Nama mugi, nama gome, nama tamago. *Raw wheat, raw rice, raw egg—Japanese*

Dii dii thii Billy Lee bilii. *These four horses are Billy Lee's horses.—Navajo*

moo mirk koong . . . moo mirk koong . . . moo mirk koong. *Pig, squid, shrimp—Thai*

Khrai khaii khai gai. *Who sells chicken eggs?—Arabic*

Ganan geedel dagan bagan, dagan gadol gadal bagan. *A gardner grew oats in a garden; the oat grew in the garden.—Hebrew*

U perepela i perepëlki pjat' perepeljat (**У перепела и перепёлки пять перепелят**). *A quail and a female quail have five little quails—Russian*

171

Caanaan caboo biyo kama daban kaban karo. *I had milk and can't have water afterwards.—Somali*

Si mon tonton tond ton tonton, ton tonton sera tondu. *If my uncle shaves your uncle, your uncle will be shaved.—French*

Bela kera prolajala. (**Бела кера пролајала**). *White dog started to bark. —Serbian*

Mi mamá me mima mucho. *Mom spoils me a lot.—Spanish*

Sárga bögre, görbe bögre. *Yellow mug, crooked mug.—Hungarian*

Siopao, siomai, suman. *Steamed buns, pork dumplings, rice cake.—Tagalong*

Wale watu wa liwali wala wali wa liwali. *The headman's people eat the headman's rice.—Swahili*

A big black bug bit a big black bear. *—English*

Made the big black bear bleed blood. *—English*

Un ver vert va vers un verre en verre. *A green worm goes towards a glass cup.—French*

Kale kakuku kadogo ka kaka kako wapi kaka? *Where are your chickens, brother?—Swahili*

She sells sea shells by the sea shore./The shells she sells are surely seashells./ So if she sells sea shells on the seashore, I'm sure she sells seashore shells. *—English*

Tanso sa tasa, tasa sa tanso. *Brass cups, cups of brass.—Tagalong*

Riba ribi grize rep. *One fish bites another fishes tail.—Croatian*

Toy boat. Toy boat. Toy boat.—English

Three free throws. Three free throws.—*English*

Fat frogs flying past fast.—*English*

Moose noshing much mush.—*English*

Black bug's blood.—*English*

Rubber baby buggy bumper.—*English*

Appendix III

Global Proverbs

AFRICA

Kiswahili, East Africa

- Mkaidi hafaidi hadi siku ya Idi. Haste makes waste.
- Chokochoko si njema mchague la kusema. Use words wisely.
- Haba na haba, hujaza kibaba. Little things, together, add up.
- Kila mwenye kusubiri hakosi kitu. Patience is virtue.
- Kuku mgeni hakosi kamba mguuni. A new hen always has a string tied to its leg; new people are easy to spot, and every person comes with an identity
- Lia na tabia yako usilaumu wenzako. Be responsible for your own choices; do not place blame.
- Mchezea wembe humkata mwenyewe. Someone who plays with dangerous will probably get hurt.
- Mso hili ana lile. Everyone has a purpose; no one is perfect.
- Mti hawendi ila kwa nyenzo. The right tools are needed to do a job correctly.
- Nazi mbovu harabu ya nzima. One bad coconut ruins the bunch.
- Shanuo baya pale linapokuchoma. Even a comb is called bad when it causes pain; a good person or tool becomes bad when they harm you.
- Ukali wa jicho washinda wembe. The eye is a razor; a look can send a clear message.
- Ukiona vyaelea vimeundwa. Every raft was made by somebody; everything good requires work.
- Usilaumu sisimizi sukari haimalizi. The ant can never finish all the sugar, so don't place blame on it; don't make excuses.
- Usisafirie nyota ya mwenzio. Don't guide your own ship by another's star. Every person has their own role, path, and destiny.

- Vidole vitano, kipi bora. Five fingers, which is best? Who's to say which one is better; they are all great because they work together.
- Zawadi ni tunda la moyo. A gift is a fruit from the heart. Any thought of giving counts.

East Africa, Cont.

- A big goat does not sneeze without reason. There are always smaller causes behind a greater reaction. —Kenya (1)
- An elephant never fails to carry its own tusk. Every person is responsible for his or herself. —East Africa
- An empty tin makes a lot of noise. Too much talking is trouble. —Kenya (1)
- People get fed up even with honey. Too much of a good thing can be bad. —Uganda
- The friends of our friends are our friends. —Congo (5)
- A single bracelet does not jingle. Strength lies in unity. —Congo (5)
- War has no eyes. There are no rules in war. —Swahili, East Africa (5)
- The forest has ears. Be careful what you say. —Kenya (1)
- The one who is too talkative leaves his mouth empty. Too much talking can be dangerous. —East Africa
- Whoever comes last drinks muddy water. Avoid procrastination. —Uganda
- There is no difference between mother and baby snakes; they are equally poisonous. Bad intentions, in whatever form, are harmful.—Kenya
- There is no pool that the sun cannot dry up. We are not invincible; pride is not wise. —Kenya

West Africa

- A child that goes places is wiser than an old man who stays in one village. Experience is a great teacher. —Nigeria
- A hungry man is an angry man. —Nigeria
- It is better to walk than curse the road. Time spent complaining is time wasted. —Senegal (2)
- A camel does not joke about the hump of another camel. Avoid speaking ill of another; we are all unique with purpose. —Guinea (2)
- The man who has bread now does not remember the time of famine. In the good times, do not forget to prepare for hard times. —Nigeria (2)
- A hippopotamus can be made invisible in water. Do not make assumptions. —West Africa (3)
- Rats don't dance in the cat's doorway. Avoid trouble. —West Africa (3)
- Only the thing for which you have struggled will last. We only really appreciate that which requires effort. —Yoruba (4)

- One who has been bitten by a snake lives in fear of worms. Once hurt, one can became wary or cautious. —Igbo (4)
- Fine words do not produce food. Talk only goes so far. —Nigeria (4)
- The length of a frog is known only after it's death. People and things are rarely appreciated until they are gone. —General (3)
- There can be no peace without understanding. Understanding is the first step. —Senegal (5)
- The child of an elephant will not be a dwarf. We are like that which we came from. —Yoruba (4)
- Whoever is patient with a cowrie shell will one day have thousands of them. Good things come to those who wait. —Hausa (4)
- A child who asks questions does not become a fool. No question is silly. —Ghana (4)
- Knowledge is like a baobab tree; no one can encompass it with their hands. Knowledge is priceless. —Ghana (4)
- If you are on the road to nowhere, find another road. Do not waste time with negative or uncertain paths. —Ghana (4)
- An army of sheep led by a lion can defeat an army of lions led by a sheep. —Ghana (5)
- Ugliness with a good character is better than beauty. Looks mean little compared to what is within. —Nigeria (5)
- The wealth which enslaves the owner isn't wealth. More money can bring more problems. —Yoruba (5)
- You become wise when you begin to run out of money. Things are often best learned and most appreciated during difficult times. —Ghana (5)
- The heart of the wise man lies quiet like limpid water. Peace in the heart brings peace in the mind. —Cameroon proverb (5)
- You learn how to cut down trees by cutting them down. Experience is the best teacher. —Gabon (5)

South Africa

- An elephant does not die of one broken rib. A bad choice or bad day does not necessarily spell destruction. —South Africa
- Do not laugh at the snake because it walks on its belly. All are different; uniqueness can serve each of us. —South Africa
- Sleep killed the lion. Laziness should be avoided. —South Africa
- The most beautiful fig may contain a worm. Not all things are as they appear. —Zulu (5)
- He who thinks he is leading and has no one following him is only taking a walk. Avoid overconfidence; be certain of your actions. —Malawi (5)

- To stir the water in the pond brings up the mud. Aggravating old wounds brings more trouble. —South Africa
- When the chief limps, all his subjects limp also. Whatever a role model does, will be copied. —South Africa

North Africa

- When spiders unite, they can destroy a lion. Unity is strength. —Ethiopia, (2)
- The fool speaks, the wise man listens. Too much talk is poison. —Ethiopia (5)
- A large chair does not make a king. We are not defined by our possessions. —Sudan (5)
- If you can't resolve your problems in peace, you can't solve them with war. Fighting does not solve a conflict. —Somalia (5)
- Wisdom does not come overnight. Good things require effort. —Somalia (5)
- Dine with a stranger but save your love for your family. Keep priorities in line. —Ethiopia (5)
- A fool is a wise man's ladder. Pay attention and be proactive. —Eritrea (7)
- When a road is good, it is used a second time. If it works, don't try to fix it. —Eritrea (7)
- Dreamers remember their dreams when they are in trouble. Preparedness is a virtue. —Eritrea (7)
- Silence is the door of consent. Speaking the mind leads to liberation —Libya (6)
- Maliciously acquired gold never lasts long. That which comes dishonestly is worthless. —Libya (6)
- If you plant olives but do not prune the tree, your oil will be good for only donkeys. Good things come with effort. —Libya (6)
- A fly that doesn't heed advice usually follows the corpse into the grave. Ignoring valuable advice can be costly. —Eritrea (7)

EAST ASIA

- *gak-naam-wa-pheuua-laaeng.* Do not use all your water before the drought. Be wise with savings. —Thailand (10)
- *gwaang neung saawk yaao neung waa naa neung kheuup.* Everyone deserves respect. —Thailand (10)
- *gaaw laaeo dtawng saan.* Do not do something halfway. —Thailand (10)
- *gam phaaeng mee huu bpra dtuu mee data.* The walls have ears, the doors have eyes. Be wise in your words and actions. —Thailand (10)

- *khit laaeo jeung jaehn ra jaa.* A word is like a rock- once you throw it, you cannot take it back. —Thailand (10)
- *deern dtaam phuu yai maa mai gat.* Be like the elders. Follow good examples. —Thailand (10)
- *Zaga ne, yan ze.* *"Less talk, less enemies." Words can cause problems.* —Burma (11)
- *Pyinna shwe o, lu ma ko.* *"Education is like a golden pot nobody can steal."*—Burma (11)
- *Damya kaung sa ta manet.* "The fruits of a theft last only a single morning." Something gained without integrity has little value. —Burma (9)
- *Yin lauk hman hma, du lauk kya hma.* "Aim for the chest to reach the knees". Always aim high. —Burma (9)
- *Kaung hmu ta khu nei zin pyu. Do something good each day. —Burmese (9)*
- *Thit ta bin kaung, hnget ta thaung.* "One sturdy tree can support ten thousand birds." It is important to build strong foundations. —Burma (9)
- *Alot ma shi kyaung yeicho.* "Bathe the cat because you have no work to do." Avoid laziness. —Burma (9)
- *pa ta chet anet hse htwei.* The same word can have many meanings. How a person says something is as important as what is actually being said. —Burma (9)
- *Nói trước bước không qua.* If you brag, also be prepared to fail. —Vietnam (8)
- *Chó cậy gần nhà, gà cậy gần chuồng*—The dog is cocky near his home, the rooster is proud near his coop. We feel most secure in our own zones of comfort. —Vietnam (8)
- *Đói cho sạch, rách cho thơm*—Endure hunger with a noble heart; own nothing, but remain clean. Moral value, culture and tradition are of key value. —Vietnam (8)

ARABIC

- أحضر الناس جواباً من لم يغضب. "The best answer will come from the person who is not angry." Find calm before acting or speaking. —Arabic (12)
- إذا تم العقل نقص الكلام. Wise people talk little. Talk can cause trouble. —Arabic (12)
- أرى كل إنسان يرى عيب غيره ويعمى عن العيب الذي هو فيه. Before judging others, judge yourself. —Arabic (12)
- أشد الفاقة عدم العقل. "Lack of intelligence is the greatest poverty." In education lies power. —Arabic (12)
- الصبر تنل. Patience is virtue. —Arabic (12)
- أول الشجرة بذرة. Even a tree must start as a seed. Every effort begins somewhere. —Arabic (12)

- اول الغضب جنون وآخره ندم. "Anger begins with madness, but ends in regret." Avoid speaking or acting from emotion. —Arabic (12)
- حبل الكذب قصير. "The rope of lies is short." The truth will soon be found out. —Arabic (12)
- تجري الرياح بما لا تشتهي السفن. "Winds blow counter to what the ship wants." We can't always get what we want. —Arabic (12)

CENTRAL ASIA

Nepal, India, Tibet

- *Pahile gerera dekhaunu ani bhannu.* Act first; tell about it after. —Nepal (16)
- *Sun Lai Khol Launu Pardaina.* Gold always seems to shine. —Nepal (16)
- *Achano ko pir khukuri le jandaina.* The knife is not concerned with how the board feels. A person who causes harm is not empathetic. —Nepal (16)
- *Afu namari swarka dekhinna.* We will only know the heavens when it is our time to reach them; we cannot judge until we've walked in another's shoes. —Nepal *2
- *Akabari sun lai kasi lagaunu pardaina.* True gold does not need to be polished (If it isn't broken, don't fix it). —Nepal (16)
- *Ek le thuki suki, saya le thuki nadi.* One spit dries but hundreds can make a river. More can be accomplished through team effort. —Nepal (16)
- *khane mukh lai junga le chekdaina.* A moustache cannot block a mouth that wants to eat. A determined person cannot be stopped. —Nepal (16)
- *Naachna najanne agan tedho.* A person who is bad at dancing will blame the floor. It is best to take responsibility for the self. —Nepal (16)
- *Baadar ko haatma nariwal.* "A coconut in a monkey's hand." If something is fragile or precious, do not be careless with it. —Nepal (16)
- *Door ke dhol suhavane lagte hain*—The drums sound more impressive from afar. The grass is greener on the other side of the fence. —India/ Hindi (17)
- *Garajne wale badal baraste nahin hain.* The one who talks the most is the least likely to produce results; actions speak louder than words. —India/ Hindi (17)
- *Ghar ka bhedi, lanka dhayey.* The one closest to you knows the most, and is the most dangerous. —India/Hindi (17)
- *Vainsh apana singon ka wajan mahasus nahi karta.* A buffalo does not feel the weight of its own horns. People are used to carrying their own burdens. —India (18)

- Pearls are worthless in the desert. The right tools for any job are essential. —India (18)
- Regularity is the best medicine. Practice makes perfect. —Hindi (18)
- Dig your well before you are thirsty. Be prepared. —Hindi (18)
- People don't trip on mountains, but they sometimes stumble on stones. Getting stuck on the small things can be detrimental. —Hindi (18)
- By saving the mustard seeds in your hand, you miss out on getting a watermelon. Do not lose sight of the big picture. —Kashmir (18)
- A simple meal at home is better than an elaborate one while away. The everyday occurrences are often the most precious. —Kashmir (18)
- The innocent often pay for the acts of the guilty. The irresponsible acts cause trouble and inconvenience to others. —Kashmir (18)
- It requires lots of time to build a good name, but only a little time to ruin it. A good reputation should be guarded. —Bengal (18)
- The owl is small, but its voice is loud. Every small contribution helps. —Tamil (18)
- Something done at the wrong time should be considered not done. There is a right time for everything. —Sanskrit (18)

Afghanistan, Pakistan

- Be beautiful from within, and your world will also be beautiful. Act in good ways, good will follow. —Afghanistan (19)
- Pleasures are wonderful, but they cannot equal milk. Money cannot buy happiness. —Pakistan
- A fool will bring harm to brave men. The thoughtless words or actions of one can jeopardize many. —Pakistan (19)
- When one camp migrates, another will follow. People will be followers. —Pakistan (19)
- The cub of a wolf will one day grow into a wolf. A thing is what it is. —Afghanistan (19)
- A friend will make you cry; an enemy will make you laugh. True friends tell you even what you don't want to hear. —Pakistan (19)
- One who has never tended sheep might know the sound of the animal's feet. Even one who has never actually done something might know something useful about it. —Afghanistan (19)

Russia, Tajikistan

- *Avval andisha ba'd guftor.* Think before talking. —Tajikistan (20)
- *Bo moh shini - moh shavi.* If you sit with the moon you become the moon. We become like that which we surround ourselves with. —Tajikistan (20)

- Больше слушай, меньше говори. Listen much, talk less. Choose your words wisely. —Russian (21)
- Без муки нет науки. Struggle is a fine teacher. —Russian (21)
- Many hands together make the work easy. —Russian (21)
- If you want to ride, you must also be willing to pull the sleigh. Great things require effort. —Russian (21)
- An enemy will agree, but a friend will argue. —Russian Proverb

AMERICAS

- *A buen hambre no hay mal pan.* For strong hunger there's no bad bread; the one who receives a gift should not complain. —Colombia (13)
- Although the monkey might dress in silk, monkey it still is. The nature of something cannot be disguised. —Puerto Rico (15)
- *A los amigos uno los escoge; los parientes son a huevo.* Friends are chosen, but family is destiny, from the beginning. —Mexico (13)
- *A mal tiempo, buena cara.* In a bad time, maintain a happy face; be positive. (13)
- *Abejas que tienen miel tienen aguijón.* Bees with honey have stingers; looks can be deceiving. —Mexico (13)
- The monkey knows the tree it climbs. The one who knows it best is the one who lives it every day. Puerto Rico (15)
- *Allí tampoco atan los perros con longaniza(s).* There they don't tie dogs with sausages either. The same is true all over the world. (13)
- *A quien dan no escoge.* One who receives a gift should not complain. (13)
- *As aparências enganam.*—Things are not always as they appear. —Brazil (14)
- *A pressa é inimiga da perfeição.* Good things come from patience. —Brazil (14)
- *Amizade é amizade, negócios à parte.* Friends are friends, business is business. —Brazil (14)
- *Quem tem boca vai a Roma.* The one who asks for help finds the way (to Rome). —Brazil (14)

EUROPE

- Non semper erit aesta. Summer is not forever. Preparation is advised. —Latin proverb
- A tree falls the way it leans. —Bulgarian Proverb

- A lie travels round the world while truth is putting her boots on. —French Proverb
- A little too late, is much too late. —German Proverb
- A loan though old is not gift. —Hungarian Proverb
- A dimple on the chin, the devil within. —Gaelic Proverb
- A clear conscience is a soft pillow. —German Proverb
- A friend in need is a friend indeed. —English Proverb
- A friend's eye is a good mirror. —Irish Proverb
- A hedge between keeps friendship green. —French Proverb
- A hen is heavy when carried far. —Irish Proverb
- A closed mouth catches no flies. —Italian Proverb

Bibliography

CHAPTER 1

American Immigration Council (2013). Located at americanimmgrationcouncil.org. Retrieved Oct. 2012.

Russell, S.S., (2002). *Refugees: Risks and Challenges Worldwide.* Migration Policy Institute, 1946–4037.

Hamilton, R. & D. Moore, (2004). *Education of Refugee Children: Documenting and Implementing Change.* In *Educational Interventions for Refugee Children*, eds R. Hamilton & D. Moore, London, UK: RoutledgeFalmer, Chapter 8.

McBrien, J.L., (2003). A Second Chance for Refugee Students. *Educational Leadership,* Vol. 61, No. 2, 76–79 O. Educational Needs and Barriers for Refugee Students in the United States: A Review of Literature. *Review of Educational Research,* Vol. 75, No. 3, 329–64.

United Nations, High Commissioner for Refugees (2012). United Nations Communications and Public Information Service, Geneva, Switzerland. Located at unhcr. org. Retrieved Aug. 2015.

McBrien, J.L., (2003). Educational Needs and Barriers for Refugee Students in the United States: A Review of Literature. *Review of Educational Research,* Vol. 75, No. 3, 329–64.

Patrick, E., (2004). *The U.S. Refugee Resettlement Program.* Migration Policy Institute, Washington, D.C. Located at migrationpolicy.org/article/us-refugee-resettlement-program. Retrieved Aug. 2015.

United Nations Convention related to the Status of Refugees (1951). *UN Article 1.* Located at unhcr.org. Retrieved Jun. 2011.

International Refugee Committee (2015). *SOAR,* New York, rescue.org, quoting United Nations Convention related to the Status of Refugees, Article 1, 1951. Retrieved Aug. 2015.

Van Hahn, N., (2002). *Annual Report to Congress—Executive Summary.* Office of Refugee Resettlement. Located at acf.hhs.gov. Retrieved Dec. 2010.

Edwards, J.R. Jr. (2012). *Religious Agencies and Refugee Resettlement.* Center for Immigration Studies. Memorandum, March 2012.

United Nations High Commissioner for Refugees (2012). United Nations Communications and Public Information Service, Geneva, Switzerland. Located at unhcr. org. Retrieved Aug. 2015.

U.S. Committee for Refugees & Immigrants (USCRI) (2015). Arlington, Va., refugees.org. Retrieved Aug. 2015.

United States Citizenship and Immigration Services (USCIS) (2013). *Path to Citizenship.* Located at uscis.gov. Retrieved Aug. 2015.

United Nations High Commissioner for Refugees (2012). United Nations Communications and Public Information Service, Geneva, Switzerland. Located at unhcr. org. Retrieved Aug. 2015.

United States Citizenship and Immigration Services (USCIS) (2013). *Path to Citizenship.* Located at uscis.gov. Retrieved Aug. 2014.

International Refugee Committee (2015). SOAR, New York. Located at rescue.org. Retrieved Aug. 2015.

U.S. Committee for Refugees & Immigrants (USCRI) (2015). Arlington, Va. Located at refugees.org. Retrieved July 2013.

Patrick, E., (2004). *The U.S. Refugee Resettlement Program.* Migration Policy Institute, Washington, D.C. Located at migrationpolicy.org/article/us-refugee-resettlement-program. Retrieved May. 2013.

CHAPTER 2

Crawford, J., (1992). *Language Loyalties, Historical Roots of U.S. Language Policy.* University of Chicago Press, Chicago.

Cambourne, B., (1995). Toward an Educationally Relevant Theory of Literacy Learning: Twenty Years of Inquiry. *The Reading Teacher,* Vol. 49, No. 3.

Baron, D., (2011). *English Spoken Here? What the 2000 Census Tells Us About the USA.* Located at english.illinois.edu. Retrieved Aug. 2011.

Tse, L., (2001). *Why Don't They Learn English? Separating Fact from Fallacy in the U.S. Language Debate.* New York Teachers College Press.

Brown, Douglas H., (2006). *Principals of Language Learning and Teaching (5th Edition).* Pearson Education ESL.

CHAPTER 3

Anderson, A., Hamilton, R., Moore, D.W., Loewen, S., & Frater-Mathieson, K., (2004). *Education of Refugee Children: Theoretical Perspectives and Best Practice.* In *Educational Interventions for Refugee Children: Theoretical Perspectives and Implementing Best Practice,* eds R. Hamilton & D. Moore, (pp. 1–11). London UK: RoutledgeFalmer.

Daud, A., Britt af Klinteberg & Per-Anders Rydelius (2008). Resilience and Vulnerability Among Refugee Children of Traumatized Parents. *Child and Adolescent Psychiatry and Mental Health*, Vol. 2(1), No. 7.

Anderson, A., (2004). *Issues of Migration, in Educational Interventions for Refugee Children,* eds R. Hamilton & D. Moore, (pp. 64–82). London UK: RoutledgeFalmer.

Frater-Matheson, K., (2004). *Refugee Trauma, Loss and Grief: Implications For intervention.* In *Educational Interventions for Refugee Children* eds R. Hamilton & D. Moore, (pp. 12–34). London: RoutledgeFalmer.

McBrien, J.L., (2003). A Second Chance for Refugee Students. *Educational Leadership* Vol. 61, No. 2, 76–9 O.

Ahearn, L.M., (2011). *The Socially Charged Life of Language, in Living Language: An Introduction to Linguistic Anthropology,* Wiley-Blackwell, Oxford, UK.

Triad Mental Health. *The Five Major Categories of Mental Illness.*

Kuglar, E.G. & Olga Acosta Price (2009). Go Beyond the Classroom to Help Immigrant and Refugee Students. *Phi Delta Kappan*, Vol. 91, No. 3, 48–52.

Dr. Oberg K., (1954). *Culture Shock and the Problem of Adjustment to the New Cultural Environments.* World Wide Classroom Consortium for International Education & Multicultural studies, 2009.

Loewen, S., (2004). Second Language Concerns for Refugee Children. In *Educational Interventions for Refugee Children,* eds R. Hamilton & D. Moore, London: RoutledgeFalmer.

Berry, J.W. & P.R. Dasen, (Eds) (1974). *Culture and Cognition: Readings in Cross-Cultural Psychology.* London: Methuen & Co.

Neimeyer, G.J. & F. Zaken-Greenberg, (1988). The Specificity of Social-Cognitive Schemas in Interpersonal Relationships. *International Journal of Personal Construct Psychology*, 1, 139–50.

Mehan, H. & L. Hubbard, I. Villaneuva, (1994). Forming Academic Identities: Accommodation Without Assimilation Among Involuntary Minorities. *Anthropology and Education Quarterly*, Vol. 25, No. 2, 91–117.

Krashen, Stephen D., (1981). *Second Language Acquisition and Second Language.* University of Southern California. Pergamon Press.

Ferfolja, T. & M. Vickers, (2010). *Supporting Refugee Students in School Education in Greater Western Sydney.* School of Education, University of Western Sydney, Critical Studies in Education, Vol. 51, No. 2, 149–62.

Guo, Y., (2006). *Why Didn't They Show Up? Rethinking ESL Parent Involvement in K-12 Education.* TESL Canada Journal Vol 24, No.1.

Ioga, C., (1995). *The Inner Workings of the Immigrant Child.* Mahwa NJ: Lawrence Erlbaum & Associates.

Treuba, Enrique T., (2000). *Immigrant Voices: In Search of Educational Equity.* Maryland: Rowman & Littlefield.

Virtue, David C., (2009). *Serving the Needs of Immigrant and Refugee Adolescents.* Principal Publishing, Reston, Va., Vol. 89, No. 1, 64–65.

DeCapua, A. & W. Smathers, F. Tang, (2009). *Meeting the Needs of Students With Limited or Interrupted Schooling: A Guide for Educators.* University of Michigan Press.

Anderson, A., (2004). *Resilience*. In *Educational Interventions for Refugee Children: Theoretical Perspectives and Implementing Best Practice*, eds R. Hamilton & D. Moore, (pp. 53–63). London: RoutledgeFalmer.

CHAPTER 4

Hamilton, R. & D. Moore, (2004). Schools, Teachers and Education of Refugee Children, In *Educational Interventions for Refugee Children: Theoretical Perspectives and Implementing Best Practice*, eds R. Hamilton & D. Moore, London: RoutledgeFalmer.

No Child Left Behind Act 3302, Section E (2015). U.S. Department of Education. Located at www2.ed.gov/policy/elsec/leg/esea02/pg50.html. Retrieved Feb 2015.

No Child Left Behind Act. U.S. Department of Education. Located at www2.ed.gov/policy/elsec/leg/esea02/pg50.html. Retrieved Feb 2015.

Bridging Refugee Youth & Childrens Services (BRYCS) (2007). *Involving Refugee Parents in Their Children's Education*. Located at brycs.org. Retrieved May 2014.

Chadha, N.K. (PhD) (2015). *Intergenerational Relationships: An Indian Perspective*. Department of Pyschology, University of Delhi. Located at un.org. Retrieved Aug 2015.

Detzner, D., (2010). *Background on South East Asian Parenting*. College of Human Ecology, University of Minnesota Press.

Hamilton, R. & D. Moore, (2004). *Schools, Teachers and Education of Refugee Children*. In *Educational Interventions for Refugee Children: Theoretical Perspectives and Implementing Best Practice*, eds R. Hamilton & D. Moore, London: RoutledgeFalmer.

Kuglar, E., (2009). *Partnering with Parents and Families to Support Immigrant and Refugee Children at School*. Center For Health & Health Care In Schools, Issue Brief No. 2.

Tse, L., (2001). *Why Don't they Learn English? Separating Fact from Fallacy in the U.S. Language Debate*. New York Teachers College Press.

Loewen, S., (2004). *Second Language Concerns for Refugee Children*. In *Educational Interventions for Refugee Children*, eds R. Hamilton & D. Moore, (pp. 35–52). London: RoutledgeFalmer.

Ng, E., *Supporting Families and Developing Parent Leaders Among the Immigrant Chinese Community in Boston*. In VUE Journal, Annenberg Institute for School Reform, pp. 38–46. Located at annenberginstitute.org. Retrieved Aug 2015.

Virginia Department of Education, Division of Instruction (2006). *English: Strategies for Teaching Limited English Proficient (LEP) Students*. Located at doe.virginia.gov. Retrieved May 2012.

Moore, D., Conceptual Policy Issues, *In Educational Interventions for Refugee Children: Theoretical Perspectives and Implementing Best Practice*, eds Richard Hamilton & Dennis Moore, London: RoutledgeFalmer.

CHAPTER 5

Virtue, David C. (2009). *Serving the Needs of Immigrant and Refugee Adolescents.* Principal, VA. Vol. 89, No. 1 64–65 S/O

Moore, D. (2004). *Conceptual Policy Issues.* In *Educational Interventions For Refugee Children,* eds R. Hamilton & D. Moore, (p. 93). London: Routledge Falmer.

Loewen, S. (2004). Second Language Concerns for Refugee Children. In *Educational Interventions for Refugee Children,* eds R. Hamilton & D. Moore, (pp. 35–52). London: RoutledgeFalmer.

Charny, J. (2008). *World Refugee Day: Where are the World's Hidden Refugees?* Refugees International. Located at https://www.refugeesinternational.org/blog/world-refugee-day-where-are-worlds-hidden-refugees. Retrieved Feb 2014.

Meyer, E. (2014). *The Culture Map: Breaking Through the Invisible Boundaries of Global Business.* Public Affairs Publishing.

Morrison, T. & Wayne A. Conaway (2006). *Kiss, Bow, or Shake Hands,* Adams Media.

Storti, C. (2007). *The Art of Crossing Cultures* (2nd Edition). International Press.

Lustig, Myron W. & J. Koester. (2009). *International Competence: Interpersonal Communication Across Cultures* (6th Edition). Pearson Publishing.

Lewis, Richard D. (2005). *When Cultures Collide: Leading Across Cultures.* (3rd Edition): Nicholas Brealey Publishing.

CHAPTER 6

McCracken, Janet B., (1993). *Valuing Diversity in the Primary Years.* National Institute for the Education of the Young, Washington DC.

Loewen, S., (2004). *Second Language Concerns for Refugee Children.* In *Educational Interventions for Refugee Children,* eds R. Hamilton & D. Moore, (pp. 35–52). London: RoutledgeFalmer.

Bhattacharjee, Y., (2012). *Why Bilinguals are Smarter,* New York Times. Located at nyt.com. Retrieved June 2015.

Examined Existence (2015). *12 Benefits of Learning A Foreign Language.* Examinedexistence.com. Retrieved July 2015.

Dotson, J.M., (2000). *Cooperative Learning Structures Can Increase Student Achievement.* West Virginia: Fairmont.

Kagan, S., (1994). *Cooperative Learning.* Kagan Publishing, California: San Clemente.

Ridley, L., (2003). *The Refugee Experience.* The Spring Insitute, Denver.

Elliot, D. & U. Segal, (2012). *Refugees Worldwide, Vol 1: Global Perspectives.* Praeger Publishing.

Collet, B. Sites of Refuge: Refugees, Religiosity, and Public Schools in the United States. *Educational Policy,* Vol. 24, No. 1, 189–215.

CHAPTER 7

Kazin, B., Principal, Place Bridge Academy, Refugee Magnate school in Denver, Colorado. *Interview*, August 17, 2015.

Hakuta, K., ButlHakuta, K., Butler, Y.G., & Witt, D., (2000). *How Long does it take English Learners to Attain Proficiency?* Located at from: http://lmri.ucsb.edu/publications/00_hakuta.pdf. Retrieved March 2010.

Burden, P. & D. Byrd, (2003). *Methods for Effective Teaching: Meeting the Needs of All Students* (5th Edition) Pearson Education.

Kaser, Catherine Hoffman, M.A., (2014). *Classroom Environment*. Old Dominion University. Located at https://www.odu.edu/content/dam/odu/col-dept/cdse/docs/1-classroom-environments.pdf. Retrieved March 2015.

Arizona Department of Education (2011). *English Language Learner Guide for Local Educational Agencies*. Located at azed.gov. Retrieved Oct 2012.

Herrell, A.L. & M.L. Jordan, (2012). *Fifty Strategies for Teaching English Language Learners* (4th Edition). Pearson Publishing.

Blachowicz, C., Fisher, P., Ogle, D. & Watts-Taffe, S., (2013). *Teaching Academic Vocabulary K-8: Effective Practices across the Curriculum*. New York: Guilford Press.

Piaget, J. (1962). *Play, Dreams and Imitation in Childhood*. New York.

Stewig & Buege, (1994). *Dramatizing Literature in Whole Language Classrooms*. New York: Teachers College Press.

CHAPTER 8

Haynes, J., (2007). *Getting Started with English Language Learners: How Educators can Meet the Challenge*. Alexandria, VA: Association for Supervision and Curriculum Development.

VanPatten, B. & A.G. Benati, (2010). *Key Terms in Second Language Acquisition*. London: Continuum.

Cummins, J., (1981). Empirical and Theoretical Underpinnings of Bilingual Education. *The Journal of Education,* Vol. 163, No. 1, 16–29.

CHAPTER 9

Cash, R.M., Ed.D (2010). *Advancing Differentiation: Thinking and Learning for the 21st Century*. Free Spirit Publishing.

Lai, Emily R., (2011). *Critical Thinking: A Literature Review. Research Report*. Pearson Publishing. Located at images.pearsonassessments.com/images/tmrs/CriticalThinkingReviewFINAL.pdf. Retrieved Feb. 2015.

Trilling, B. & C. Fadel, (2007). *21st Century Skills: Learning for Life in Our Times* (1st Edition). Jossey-Bass.

Partnerships for 21st Century Learning (2009). *P21 Framework Definitions*. Located at p21.org. Retrieved July 2011.

Van Briesen, Jeanne M., (2009). Oral presentation for Department of Civil and Environmental Engineering Carnegie Mellon University. Located at nae.edu. Retrieved May 2015.

Hay, I., & N. Dempster, (2004). *Student Leadership Development within a School Curriculum Framework*. In Bartlett, B., Bryer, F., & Roebuck, D. (Eds) Education: *Weaving Research into Practice*. International Language, Cognition and Special Education Conference, Gold Coast, Vol. 2, 141–50.

Branson, Margaret S. (1989). *International and Citizenship Education: Need and Nexus*. Paper presented at the International Conference on Constitutional Government and the Development of an Enlightened Citizenry, Los Angeles, CA. ED 314 302.

Iowa Department of Education (2010). *Iowa Core K-12 21st Century Skills: Essential Concepts and Skills with Details and Examples*. Located at https://www.educateiowa.gov/sites/files/ed/documents/K-12_21stCentSkills_0.pdf. Retrieved May 2014.

Cain, J., M. Cummings & J. Stanchfie, (2005). *A Teachable Moment: A Facilitator's Guide to Activities for Processing, debriefing, Reviewing and Reflection* (1st Edition). Kendall Hunt Publishing.

McGonigal, J., (2011). *Reality is Broken: Why Games Make Us Better and How They can Change the World* (1st Edition). Penguin Press.

Jacobson, E., (2014). *Research Roundup: Studies Support Game-based Learning*. Located at https://www.filamentgames.com/research-roundup-studies-support-game-based-learning. Retrieved Feb. 2015.

Breuer, B., (2010). Eludamos, *Journal for Computer Game Culture*, Vol. 4, No. 1, 7–24.

Kapp, Karl M. (2013). *Goals in Learning: The Gamification of Learning and Instruction*. Pfeiffer Publishing.

Shelton, Brett E. & J. Scoresby (2011). *Aligning Game Activity with Educational goal: Following a Constrained Design Approach to Instructional Computer Games*. Utah. Located at Educational Technology Research and Development. Retrieved October 2012.

Thompson, D., et al. (2012). In Pursuit of Change: Youth Response to Intensive Goal Setting Embedded in a Serious Video Game. *J Diabetes Sci Technol*. 2007 Vol. 1, No. 6, 907–17.

McGonigal, J., (2011). *Reality is Broken: Why Games Make Us Better and How they can Change the World* (1st Edition). Penguin Press.

McClarty, et al. (2012). *A Literature Review of Gaming Education*. Pearson Publishing.

Sander B., C. Tien Tan & Y. Pisan, (2012). *Personalised Gaming: A Motivation and Overview of Literature*. Auckland, New Zealand. Located at sander.landodsand/publications. Retrieved Aug. 2015.

Fanning Ruth M. & D.M. Gaba (2007). *The Role of Debriefing in Simulation Based Learning*. University Medical School at Stanford, Vol. 2, No. 2.

Bill and Melinda Gates Foundation (2015). *Press Release: Gates Foundation Announces Portfolio of Innovative Grants to Develop New Teaching and Learning Tools that Support Teachers and Help Students.* Located at gatesfoundation.org. Retrieved June 2015.

Ulisack, M. (2010). *Games in Education: Serious Games.* Future Lab UK. Located at media.futurelab.org.uk/resources/documents/lit_reviews/Serious-Games_Review.pdf. Retrieved July 2, 2015.

Gates, B. Written testimony of Bill Gates before Committee on Science and Technology, U.S. House of Representatives: http://www.sciencedebate2008.com/www/index.php?id=27.

Wang, J., (PhD) (2014). *Planet Hunters, A Zooniverse Project Blog.* Located at http://blog.planethunters.org/category/planets. Retrieved June 2014.

APPENDICES

Mbit, John S. (1991). *An Introduction to African Religions.* Heinemann Publishing, South Africa.

Kajenbi (2014). Kajenbi.com/African-proverbs.html.

Jones, Crbs (2014). umd.edu, 2014

Boston University African Study Center (2014). http://www.bu.edu/africa/

Mawuna Koutonin (2014). SiliconAfrica,

History of Painters (2014). historyofpainters.com

African Proverbs in African Literature (2014). Wordpress, https://proverbsafricanliterature.wordpress.com/country-profile/southern-africa/mozambique/

Khaithu at Wordpress (2014). https://khaithu.wordpress.com

Kyaw, A., Zagabon (2014). http://zagabon.tumblr.com/about

Thai-language.com (2014). 2014 thai-language.com.

Kyaw, Aung Htin (2014). Fifty Viss, Burma Language.

Udemy Online Schools (2013). Udemy.com/blog/Arabic-proverbs/

The Language Realm (2014). http://www.languagerealm.com

Aryel Lanes (2014). http://www.aryellanes.com/2014_06_01_archive.html

Puerto Rico Channel, Puertorico.com (2014). NewMedi Holdings, Inc.

Nepalgo (2014). Nepalgo@Tumblr

Indif Technologies (2014). Infif.com

Ohebsion, Rodney (2014). Huffinton Post

Mphil, T. Kinnes (2014). http://oaks.nvg.org.

Eichner, Kyle (2014). Fulbright ETA, omukhtan.blogspot.com

MasterRussian (2004). http://masterrussian.net/f14/translation-todays-picture-masterrussian-com-918/

Index

About the Author

Louise H. Kreuzer is an active Denver educator with extensive experience in ELA-E and ELD curriculum, instruction, and design. She has been teaching in refugee and Newcomer settings for nearly a decade. Louise was honored as a Rodel Exemplary Student Teacher in 2007 and a Denver Teacher of the Year in 2012. Louise also served as a United States Professional Fulbright agent to Tanzania in 2010, where she extensively studied and reported on refugee crises, with a focus on community-wide educational consequences. In this realm, Louise thoroughly investigated and detailed the effects of post-traumatic stress on pre-settlement refugees; and subsequently, the effects of PTSD on post-resettlement transition and learning.

Following the Fulbright study, Louise returned to East Africa repeatedly. There, she founded a nonprofit, established a no-cost school, and utilized Swahili to train local educators in heading academic efforts at the compound. The school remains active, graduating its first class in 2013.

In her local community, Louise has established herself as an active liaison and occasional interpreter between refugee housing communities and the school.

Made in the USA
Columbia, SC
30 January 2021